Troubling Dreams

Dear Nancy,

May your dreams
trust and guide you
all the deep of your life
and may you know from
along the way.

Sandi E. Shook, Ph.D.

Troubling Dreams
Unlocking the Door to Self-Awareness

By
Sadie E. Strick, Ph.D.

New Horizon Press
Far Hills, New Jersey

From *Animal-Speak: The Spiritual & Magical Powers of Creatures Great & Small,* by Ted Andrews. Copyright 2005. Used by permission of Llewellyn Publications.

From *Animal Wise: The Spirit Language and Signs of Nature,* by Ted Andrews. Copyright 1999. Used by permission of Dragonhawk Publishing.

From Business and Professional Women's Survey/USA, Pay Equity. Copyright 2005. Used by permission of Business and Professional Women's Foundation.

From *Goddesses in Older Women* by Jean Shinoda Bolen. Copyright 2001. Used by permission of HarperCollins Publishers.

From *An Illustrated Encyclopaedia of Traditional Symbols,* by J.C. Cooper. Copyright 1978. Used by permission of Thames and Hudson Ltd, London.

From "Voudoun ('Voodoo'): The Religious Practices of Southern Slaves in America," by Mamaissii "Zogbé" Vivian Hunter-Hindrew, Hounon Amengansie. Copyright 2007. Used by permission of author.

From *The Way of Individuation,* by Jolande Jacobi. Translated by RFC Hull. Copyright 1967. Used by permission of Houghton Mifflin Harcourt.

Strick, Sadie E.
Troubling Dreams: Unlocking the Door to Self-Awareness
Cover design: Wendy Bass
Interior design: Susan Sanderson and Charley Nasta

Library of Congress Control Number: 2011923115

ISBN 13: 978-0-88282-366-9
New Horizon Press

Manufactured in the U.S.A.

15   14   13   12   11   1   2   3   4   5

For
Carol Morse Kline,

whose dedication to the education
of mature women made it all possible

AUTHOR'S NOTE

This book is about the challenges that women face in their everyday lives in the workplace, home and society. Most importantly, this book honors the women who have dared to take the necessary risks to embrace and own their authentic selves. These women have left bread-crumbs on the path, a map to inform our travels and show us the courageous journey from despair to personal empowerment.

This book is based on the author's research, personal experiences and clients' real-life experiences. The identities of the subjects of this book have been altered to ensure confidentiality. Names have been changed and identifying characteristics have been altered except for contributing experts.

For purposes of simplifying usage, the pronouns he/she and him/her are sometimes used interchangeably. The information contained herein is not meant to be a substitute for professional evaluation and therapy with mental health professionals.

CONTENTS

INTRODUCTION...1

CHAPTER 1   Women's Disturbing Issues.................................5

CHAPTER 2   Dreams and Dreaming...................................13

CHAPTER 3   Addiction...19

CHAPTER 4   Depression...57

CHAPTER 5   Harassment..81

CHAPTER 6   Job Stress..99

CHAPTER 7   Digestive Disorders...143

CHAPTER 8   Anger...151

CHAPTER 9   Panic Attacks..161

CONCLUSION...211

NOTES..221

ACKNOWLEDGEMENTS...225

Introduction

Dream analysis is an essential part of the psychotherapy process. To solve any problem, we need all the available information. Without the dream there is only limited information with which to work. What we know in our conscious minds is limited to our waking experiences. What we do not know is what lies in the unconscious and yet, what lies in the unconscious belongs to us and is very important. The unconscious mind holds memories and experiences not readily available to conscious memory. At its very deepest level, the unconscious speaks to us in the language of symbols, a universal language common to all cultures. Symbols are images that represent something else by reason of relationship, association, convention or accidental resemblance. The symbols that occur in dreams represent something that has been repressed. They are meaningful and necessary to guide the dreamer and the therapist toward healing the wounds that prevent a person from owning and embracing her authentic self.

During twenty-eight years of practicing Jungian psychotherapy, I have become acutely aware of how often the same symbols appear in the dreams of women who engage with me in psychotherapy, whether for reasons of depression, anxiety, abusive situations, marital distress, physical symptoms with no recognizable causes, work stress, chemical dependencies, poor self-esteem or codependency issues.

I have found that the Serpent symbol occurs in many women's dreams and it is the one I have focused upon with the women featured in this book. The Serpent, as a symbol, has many different meanings: It represents healing (symbolized by the physician's emblem, a staff with two serpents interweaving from the bottom and, at the top, facing each other). It also is the symbol of death and new life.

In tribal societies, animals in dreams are known as *totems* or *spirit guides*. They are sacred and each animal has a special meaning. The Serpent, in particular, is the predictor of change and the possibility of new life (symbolically, the shedding of the old skin). To meet the Serpent in dreams is to meet change.

Animals in dreams are many and varied. Each has its own special meaning and all are important to the dreamer. Whatever animal inhabits the dream is the special guide for the dreamer at the time it occurs. We are not confined to only one animal in dreams. We are given what we need and different animals will appear in our dreams, depending on the circumstances of our lives at the time. I discuss with my clients that they should think of the animal totem as a blessing, for it gives the dreamer a special energy to move forward in life. Be assured that the psyche, by way of the dream, will help us advance in the journey toward being all we can be.

This book reveals, through real-life stories, the connection between a woman's feelings of powerlessness and disturbance in mood with the appearance of a dream animal to inspire her to action on her own behalf. The notion of changing a life situation typically strikes as much terror as the image of the animal itself, especially when the animal is fierce and threatening. However, the more viciously the animal behaves, the more critical is the dreamer's need for change. To the extent that the dreamer is willing to face the challenge, work toward the resolution of the problems she is experiencing and own her authentic self, the animal changes from its frightening character to become the healing spirit guide.

Partly because of my own experiences of the benefit of psychodynamic psychotherapy and because this type of deep therapy addresses all phases of the healing process, my work focuses on dreams and the symbols contained in the dreams to promote healing, growth and personal empowerment.

The information, strategies, tools and personal histories of the women featured in this book will reveal to you, the reader and traveler on your own journey into the depths of the unconscious, the passage which needs to be undertaken to return to the authentic self. As you move forward on this journey I am confident you will become successful, empowered and ready to face the future with courage, determination and trust in yourself and in your own ability to be all you can be.

1.

Women's Disturbing Issues

Susan, a stylishly dressed single woman of thirty-five, hesitantly seated herself near my chair and shyly began to speak. Her eyes filled with tears as she told of the humiliation she was experiencing in the workplace. In the last five years, three opportunities for promotion had become available. When Susan applied for the first position, she was told that she was more valuable in the job she was currently holding. When her second attempt was denied she was told that she wasn't exactly what management had in mind for the position. The third reason for denying her an available promotion was that the chosen candidate had fresh ideas to bring to the table and the company needed new ideas. In each case, the candidate who was chosen over Susan was male. None had the advanced degrees in the subject that she held. None had been with the company for as long as she had.

Susan began thinking about why she failed in attaining her goals. What was wrong? Why was she not recognized for her contributions to the company? Could she ever hope to advance in her chosen profession? To what lengths would she have to go to prove herself deserving of a promotion? Soon she realized it was a recurring situation. She had held a similar position five years previous to her current job and left that company when she was denied a promotion on two occasions. "I feel that I am wasting my life," she reflected.

Natalie lives in a Middle Eastern country where children are betrothed at a very young age and, as adults, remain bound by this decision. If, for any reason, the woman is rejected by her future husband, she is considered to be a disgrace to her family and is no longer welcome in her parents' home. Essentially, she becomes an outcast, both in her native land and within the social community anywhere in the world. There is no place she can go and fit into the social network of her culture. Furthermore, no man of her culture would ever consider her as a candidate to become his wife and mother of his children. For the male, however, the rules differ. If he breaks the agreement, he suffers no consequences beyond a mild reprimand. He will have no problem choosing another wife. Natalie's fiancé decided against marrying her. When Natalie pleaded with her fiancé to reconsider their betrothal, he refused.

Gloria, a thirty-seven-year-old married woman and mother of one child, nervously clutched her sweater around her and made every effort to hide her shaking hands within its folds. Her eyes were swollen and barely disguised bruises were visible on her face and neck. Her voice was cautious and it seemed to be with great effort that she could speak at all. Her first words to me were, "I am afraid. He is going to kill me."

Gloria was afraid of her husband of six years. She gave a chilling account of abuse, beginning with pushing, shoving, veiled threats and jealousy and escalating to serious physical, psychological and emotional abuse. One by one her friends stopped calling, with the exception of one friend who remained steadfast. In her, Gloria confided her torments and fear for her life. Even during pregnancy the abuse continued. Gloria reasoned that once their child was born the situation would improve. In fact, it actually worsened. Her husband's favorite type of punishment was to squeeze Gloria's throat until she felt that she would stop breathing and, at those times, she hoped that she would die. During the most recent attack, the last thing she recalled before fainting was her young son screaming in terror as he witnessed the horrific sight.

Gloria felt that she could do nothing to solve this problem on her own and called on her friend and parents to help. Together, they removed her and her child from the home, taking only as many belongings as they could carry. Knowing that her child was safe with her parents, Gloria agreed to see a psychologist for guidance and came to my office. A landmark 2005 World Health Organization study showed the correlation between domestic violence and a high incidence of mental health issues.[1] The seriousness of Gloria's depression was unmistakable. I informed Gloria of the various agencies that are ready to help in these situations and on very short notice. Later that day, she and her child were safely in the hands of people who had the sympathy of the courts and the expertise and the means to help her to heal and reconstruct her life.

Maria, a charming, married woman of forty, accompanied by Jason, her husband of twelve years, came to me for help with their marital problems. Both Maria and Jason were employed in their chosen professions. Both were college graduates and happy with their careers. While Maria was very satisfied with her marriage, she had little interest in sex. In the last year, she often ended the interaction by weeping and emotionally distancing herself. Jason was concerned and caring at first but lately he found himself to be angry and frustrated with her behavior. He introduced the idea of therapy as a means of attempting to get to the root of the problem, because he was seriously contemplating divorce despite his love for her.

When she shared her background, Maria told of being abused as a child by a close, trusted family member. From age four, she was forced to keep his behavior secret under the threat that he would make her mother cry if she ever told. Her guilt was unspeakable at the thought of making her mother cry, so she kept the secret. The abuse continued until she was eight years old.

Maria's focus was on achieving excellent grades in school. She graduated with high honors and won a scholarship to the college of her choice. She had few male friends and after one attempt to engage in sex, she declined to attempt this activity again. To the world, Maria looked like a well-adjusted, studious young woman. As an adult, she had mixed feelings about her mother. She often wondered how her mother could fail to see the tension between herself and the relative who had abused her or, Maria wondered, did her mother not want to see? After she entered university, Maria had little interest in returning to or even visiting the family home.

Throughout the course of their courtship, Jason and Maria made a few attempts at fulfilling sex, which failed. They reasoned that once they were married the problem would be resolved and they entered into the marriage optimistic and happy. As time went on the problem continued and the strain on their marriage was such that they realized that they could no longer manage and agreed to seek help. Both agreed that their love for each other was worth the effort that it would take to mend the problem.

These vignettes illustrate some of the all-too-common problems women experience: sex and job discrimination in the workplace; the rights and privileges that men enjoy in different cultures of the world, as opposed to the harsh treatment of women; spousal abuse and incest committed by a trusted family member. These are not isolated problems limited to a few unfortunate women. The systematic domination of women practiced in many countries of the world is widespread. We need to take an active part in ending this tyranny.

My practice includes twenty-five to thirty-percent males. However, I believe that men are bound by social and cultural norms that have been in place for over eleven thousand years.[1] At that time, nomadic tribes roamed about in search of food. He was the hunter and she the nurturer and gatherer.[2] Together they moved from place to place to find the resources for survival. They owned nothing in the form of property or assets.

Approximately eight thousand years ago in the Middle East, tribes began to settle in one place and develop the land by planting and harvesting. What naturally followed was the development of communities and laws governing the community.[3] Property ownership appears to have been the catalyst for the change from partnership between man and woman to patriarchy (a system of government that grants men supremacy over women). With this change, the status of women changed dramatically. She no longer worked beside him as an equal. It was man's responsibility to create the conditions for survival as a landowner. Owning property and harvesting the crops created a need for workers. It is believed that slavery was introduced in response to this need. Since women and children were subject to patriarchy, some were treated as a commodity to be traded, bought and sold as slaves and were forced to labor for their masters.[4] No longer were man and woman partners. He, as patriarch, held the power and she was required to obey, subject to his authority. Religious laws were later developed that severely restricted the conduct and activities of women.[5] Today, the women of the Middle East are challenging these laws.

In the ancient world, the nature of religious worship also changed to reflect the superiority of man with the rise of Akenhaten as Pharaoh of Egypt, more than three thousand years ago. Prior to that time, the Egyptians worshiped gods and goddesses who represented nature and its creatures.[6] Akenhaten believed that there was only one god and that god was the sun. The sun was considered to be male in this type of religious practice. During his reign, Akenhaten ordered the destruction of all temples except those dedicated to Ra, the sun god,[7] essentially eliminating the depiction of the feminine as sacred. Then he declared himself to be the supreme one, the son of Ra. As formal religions began to evolve, the idea of man's superiority over women also evolved to reflect the sharp division between male and female.[8] Even though women in America have made significant gains in comparison to the women of Islam, we have yet to achieve economic and political equality with men.

What does this have to do with men in America today? It is hard to be a patriarch. It is hard to be responsible to meet the needs of employers, family and community. It is hard to be macho on the outside and sensitive on the inside! Most modern men have yet to learn how to partner with women in a fair and equitable way. They have yet to learn that it is not unmanly to be sensitive.

Customs are very difficult to change, given their enduring state in any culture. The work toward changing the customs that perpetuate the serious injustices between men and women worldwide is ahead of us. We must all, both men and women, take part in this effort. Whatever happens to one of us happens to all of us.

Women also suffer disproportionately with emotional problems. According to the National Institute of Mental Health, "Of the thirty-five million Americans suffering with depression, women outnumber men by almost two-to-one."[5] Each of the women in the prior profiles suffered from depression and anxiety, all severe enough to warrant seeking therapy and/or medical attention.

While women may be focused on their symptoms of depression, anxiety, poor health, failing marriages, estranged children, spousal abuse, feelings of abandonment when children leave home, chronic pain, work stress, excessive weight gain or loss for no apparent medical reason, history of or present experiences of rape and abuse (to name a few reasons for seeking professional help), the common denominator is feelings of fear and powerlessness. In some cases, physical pain and chronic illness can be an indicator of psychological pain, especially when no known cause is found to identify any physical problem.

People who are depressed and anxious are often subject to dreams of a disturbing nature and physical and psychological discomfort. The most widely reported symptoms among the women profiled in this book are depression, anxiety, sleep disturbance, gastrointestinal problems, back and neck pain, headaches, poor self-esteem, anger and a constant feeling of fear. The wounds they carried were sometimes based on painful childhood experiences that had never been resolved. Unresolved wounds leave us more vulnerable to the same type of situation and often we repeat these hurts with our choices of spouses and friends, because that is what we know best.

It takes incredible courage to attend to the task of righting that which is amiss in our lives. Even to engage in therapy is often a frightening experience in the beginning, but the task is to persevere and ultimately triumph over the obstacles in the way. A woman's own feeling of powerlessness represents the biggest obstacle of all. In the true stories of women with troubling dreams documented in this book, we follow the path that takes these brave women from fear, despair and helplessness to growth, renewal and empowerment. Each of the women makes her own statement about the meaning of the experience of therapy to her. The path we follow is by way of the dream.

2.

Dreams and Dreaming

Why are dreams important? We sleep, we dream, we remember, we do not remember. What's the big deal? The big deal is that everything that happens in the psyche has a purpose. Dreams contain personal and general information. They are preprogrammed and never need updating or reprogramming. Dreams have an infinite amount of usable space and never run out of ideas; what you need is what you get, more than once if necessary. They cannot be corrupted. They cannot err, lie or mislead. They are not subject to power failures, are always available to us and always in good working order. Dreams do not have boundaries to bind or restrict them. They are generous and give us their wisdom in symbolic language according to our needs. We need only to pay attention to the dream to benefit from that wisdom. Dreams are ever-present in the psyche of every man, woman and child. They are a gift from psyche to you.

Ordinary dreams are dreams that have to do with events that we experience on a daily basis. Nonetheless, they offer information on what we need to do to take the next step or resolve a problem.

Although ordinary dreams fade away quickly and do not leave a lasting impression, they still contain messages that should be addressed in the waking state. All dreams are important.

Some dreams predict the future. Predictive dreams inform us before an event happens. Many of us have heard of people who have dreamed of a plane crash prior to a scheduled flight. On the basis of the dream, they cancelled their plane tickets and, true to the warning from the dream, the plane crashed. It is important to heed warnings in dreams, especially if there is a strong feeling (in this case, a sense of foreboding) that accompanies the dream. Other predictive dreams can simply be "knowing" that the job you applied for is yours or that the new baby is going to be a boy or a girl. Predictive dreams address the future.

Some dreams compensate for what we do not have or cannot get. Imagine a person who is hungry and does not have enough food. Her dreams may very well be of a banquet with tables overflowing with food of every type and all of the food is available to her. Oh, joy! She happily eats to her heart's content. The dream is compensating for her hunger.

Recurring dreams are dreams that come back again and again with the same theme. Sometimes themes begin in childhood and recur in different forms but with similar underlying meaning throughout a lifetime. These dreams usually are concerned with unresolved problems that need to be addressed. Once the dreamer has resolved the problem, the burden is gone and the dream no longer returns.

Big dreams are those that leave a lasting impression, so much so that one remembers the dream for years. The impact is great. They have a quality that goes well beyond what we come into contact with on a daily basis. Such dreams often come at a time of crisis when major decisions must be made or major events are about to happen.

Consider the experience of Jenny, a woman whom I counseled who dreamed of a gravestone with her mother's name engraved on it. Frightened, when she awoke she immediately called her mother. She voiced her fear of the message in the dream to her mother, who laughed at the absurdity of her daughter's fears. The mother declared that she had had a medical checkup two weeks previously and she assured Jenny that she was in very good health. However, exactly four weeks later the mother suddenly became ill and died within hours, a victim of a massive heart attack.

The dream had already informed the dreamer of this impending event. The *feeling* of the dream was the clue that this was no ordinary dream. It was a *big dream*. Can we stop the event from happening? It is hard to say. In the example of cancelling a flight on the basis of a dream and the overwhelming fear that one could die a horrible death, the answer is yes. In the case of a warning of impending death from an undiagnosed cause, it depends on whether the person seeks advice medically and if the doctor takes the dream's warning seriously without evidence of symptoms and if ordered tests detect the problem. Sometimes all the tests come back negative and death occurs anyway.

With such a predictive dream, the dreamer has been forewarned and that warning is already helping her to cope with the sudden loss. Big dreams also point the way we must go or changes we must make, whether we want to or not. Psyche, by way of the dream, will let us know when it is time for change. The *feeling* that one has after a big dream is the clue that something very important is happening.

Think of a dream as a series of pictures that run by like a movie. Sometimes the characters speak and sometimes there are no spoken words. Sometimes there are no characters at all, just a landscape or an image. Dreams can even be a story with a beginning, middle and end. They have a language all their own. They speak to us in symbols.

Symbols are signs of deeper meaning. Some symbols have been in existence for thousands of years (some so ancient they cannot be traced back to their origins). There are religious symbols, such as the crucifix, a symbol of Christianity, or the Star of David, a symbol of Judaism. There are cultural symbols, such as flags, and family symbols, such as family crests. There are an infinite number of symbols and some are stored in the mind of each and every one of us at a very deep

level. They can emerge anytime and at will, especially when an important event or change is occurring or about to happen.

The presence of people in dreams is symbolic, just as objects or
landscapes are. The symbol of a man in a woman's dream is important. There are two sides to everything! The special qualities of being
a woman are the ability to *feel* the way things are and the ability to
express emotions. The special quality of being a man is the ability to
turn emotions off and see the world from a logical and rational point
of view. We need to be able to feel and speak our emotions and we
need the ability to be logical and reasonable. Symbolically, a man in a
dream is the *other* side, the side of reason and logic. He is a woman's
inner partner, her inner male. When he is kind and helpful in the
dream, it is safe to say that the dreamer is using all the resources available to her. When he is nasty, hateful and punishing, she is neglecting
to use the levelheaded part of herself, usually because she is emotionally upset and not able to be cool and concise.

The task is to get back into balance. Emotions are part of being
human, but if they are out of control and one cannot make logical
decisions, then the inner male will not be nice. The dream guides the
dreamer toward restoring balance in her life. We need it all: cool, calm,
collected reasoning and owning our feelings and insights, preferably
without losing sight of one or the other.

In tribal societies, nature and animals are revered as sacred. Animals in dreams are believed to possess sacred, symbolic meanings and
are known as *totems*.[1] Totems are the same in the culture of the tribe
as the guardian angel is to the Christian. All the animals have special
meanings of their own. They are regarded as spirit guides for the
dreamer. When an animal appears in a dream, this animal is your spirit
guide. We can have many animals that inhabit our dreams, more than
once. They can be in recurring dreams or only appear once in a lifetime. Every animal is special and important to the dreamer. It is wise
to heed the message of this very special symbol.

With the exception of one woman whose animal spirit guide was
a pack of dogs, the Serpent was the animal that most often made

its appearance in the women's dreams discussed in this book. The Serpent has many different meanings. It is an ancient symbol, often with dual meanings such as "life and death," "healing and poison" and "physical and spiritual rebirth."[2] In dreams, the Serpent most often represents a significant change that is about to occur, whether the dreamer is ready or not. It is the call to action! To the extent that the dreamer ignores or fails to take the necessary steps to overcome the obstacles in her way to health and well-being, the Serpent will appear in a frightening form, threatening and fearsome. The Serpent can be fierce, especially when the dreamer is failing to live up to her full potential. This represents its poisonous qualities. However, when the task is accomplished and the dreamer has overcome the obstacles to health, well-being and owning her authentic self, the Serpent evolves into the healing Serpent, her own special totem and spirit guide that accompanies her as she travels into the future.

Like the Serpent's ability to shed its old skin and grow a new one (symbolically, death and resurrection), the dreamer marches bravely into the future, leaving her old skin behind, confident in her ability to embrace life with grace and fortitude, making good use of all the resources available to her. This is the way of the dream.

3.

Addiction

When Alena, a twenty-nine-year-old single woman, arrived for her scheduled appointment with me, her appearance was alarming. Her face and eyes were swollen and her skin was blotchy with reddened areas, suggesting that she may have been seriously abused. I waited quietly as tears tumbled from her eyes. It was a few minutes before she gained enough control to explain she had not been abused but had been in a physical altercation with her live-in companion. Alena added that physical fights were a common occurrence of late between her and her companion, who was also a woman.

Alena was a tall woman, lean and muscular. She enjoyed and engaged in serious athletic competitions. At the time that she began her therapy, she had sustained an injury to her foot and could not compete in sports. She was worried that she might never be able to participate in her favorite sports again. As she said this, she broke down and wept again. It took minutes before she regained her composure.

Although she was functional and worked at her job as a computer analyst, Alena was struggling with an addiction to drugs and alcohol. She was able to be present at her job daily and was in no danger of losing her source of income at this time, but with the added stresses of the foot injury and serious domestic problems, she was unsure about her ability to continue to do well at her job. Just being on time was a challenge for her and, since her job was her primary source of income, the possibility of not having a job was frightening.

As we talked, I found that Alena was a very talented woman. She held a bachelor's degree in computer science and teaching and was a certified Reiki specialist. Reiki is a special form of healing originally developed in Japan that uses the hands and touching to transfer and balance the body's energies. She was also quite knowledgeable about healing through a healthy, chemical-free diet of unprocessed foods. Her goal was to promote healing and maintaining health through nutrition and exercise. Providing counsel on healthy nutrition was where Alena was most content. Unfortunately, however interesting and rewarding these occupations were to Alena, they were not profitable enough to pay the bills. Alena felt trapped in a job she no longer enjoyed, trapped in her addiction, trapped in a body that would not stop hurting and trapped in a relationship that was painful. Her family was unaware of her need for support and she elected to keep it that way for reasons she later revealed to me, leaving her essentially without a support system. All of her friends were also friends with her partner and they were choosing sides in the battle between herself and her partner. No one chose to be on her side.

In our meetings I found that Alena's opinion of herself was very poor. She often expressed feelings of self-hate and disgust, referring to herself as jealous, insecure and weak, because she was unable to make the break from her partner. It didn't help that she was being reminded daily by her partner and friends that she was mentally ill and needed help. Alena never questioned that these opinions might, in fact, be wrong. She appeared to have accepted this negative image of herself as fact. Moreover, she could not imagine that anything worthy could be included in any description of her.

Alena was the second of four children. Her younger twin sister and brother were mentally challenged. Her older brother was eight years older than she and she had little in common with him. Alena's mother was overextended and stressed with the task of caring for two young children with special needs and attending to the family in general. The burdens placed upon her mother were heavy. Her father was emotionally distant and had little input in his home life. He just drifted with the flow of things and kept isolated when he could. Nonetheless, in her childhood years Alena felt that she could talk with him and he always responded kindly to her when she approached him. He did not take an active role in any of her athletic events and, in recent years, was even less involved. Providing well for the family, he worked as an engineer and was faithful to his responsibilities in the workplace. In the home, he was silent and withdrawn.

Alena's father harbored a deep resentment of the younger children for needing so much and only interacted with them in anger. He was not abusive but reacted toward them in an angry manner for any reason, no matter how unimportant. Alena, concerned about her father's behavior and attitude toward the younger children, devoted as much time as she could to them. Alena privately felt that her mother tried to make up for the younger children's shortcomings, overcompensating to the extent that other family members, even her father, were left out of the inner circle of her mother and her special-needs children.

Gathering information on her background, I learned that in her childhood years Alena was more inclined to go to her father when he was available rather than her mother. The extent to which her father was available was determined by his moods. He had always used prescription drugs and alcohol for as long as she could remember and this significantly altered his mood if he drank too much on any given day. Her mother was intolerant of her and, if her mother was angry for whatever reason, punishment was swift and unrelenting. Alena felt her to be unapproachable most of the time. In fact, Alena described feeling estranged from all members of her family for most of her life, with the exception of her younger siblings. She took care to nurture them and they were affectionate toward her. In her adult years, Alena developed a mature understanding of her mother's dilemma and, in turn, sympathized with her. Presently, she told me she challenged her father from time to time on the subject of his lack of involvement with the family; however, he remained distant and unyielding and the family's interactions were unchanged.

As we worked together I found Alena was struggling with life at multiple levels: addiction, a failed relationship, alienation from her family, intense loneliness, work stress, economic problems, grief, loss and physical pain. She was unhappy with her job situation but felt she could not afford to change or terminate her employment. She and her partner were considering separation but neither would make the decision to actually separate. Codependency on both sides only added to the problems.

As the pressures increased, Alena's self-hate became bitter and even led to suicidal thoughts to rid herself of the horrible image of herself as unworthy and undeserving of anything but the trouble that she was experiencing. She grieved the loss of her relationships. She was very angry, but she was able to keep the intensity of the anger and pain under control. No matter how hard she tried, it was evident that she was at the end of her rope. It was as if one would light the fuse (by way of argument or criticism) and then she would explode!

This self-punishment went on for several weeks with no resolution in sight, so, since she would not or could not speak of when she began to feel so hurt and angry, I asked her to pretend that she was an artist and put her feelings down on paper. After I supplied her with paper and colored pencils, she quietly worked on her first drawing to express her feelings. The drawing was shocking! There was only blackness and chaos. Her depression could not be ignored.

For each individual, the pattern of illustrating feelings, thoughts or dream images is different. Alena could illustrate her feelings on the spot, but the illustration of a dream could be delayed by several weeks or even months. Throughout the course of her therapy, Alena drew many pictures of her feelings and dreams and she kept them neatly arranged in a folder that she carried with her.

As I studied Alena's drawings I found that the extent of Alena's depression could not be mistaken from the serious nature of these illustrations. Although I expressed my observations and concerns to her, Alena was strongly opposed to any medical solution to her depression, such as antidepressants. She firmly believed in the principles of holistic healing. We decided that Alena would use the safe expression of her feelings by way of drawings and intensive psychotherapy as her medium of treatment, so long as any tendency toward suicide was openly discussed with me and Alena took the necessary steps to prevent the loss of her life. Alena promised that she would comply with this plan.

Therapy is more than dream analysis or sharing information. It is task oriented as well. Alena had many layers of pain relating to addiction, loss, grief, isolation and codependency. She was financially responsible for herself as well. Job dissatisfaction was no small matter. She depended on her job to survive. The Reiki career was extra money but would not generate enough income to be self-supporting. Even though Alena shared much information during our meetings, she seemed restricted and unable to go beyond the obvious.

I found that Alena was most comfortable with expressing her feelings, images and dreams through art and that she invested herself in these projects in a serious, meaningful way. I attempted to help Alena trust in herself enough to *talk* about the pain she was feeling. She just couldn't go beyond the losses she was experiencing at the moment. She was often hungover after a night of drinking alcohol and she produced drawings that were chaotic and disjointed, partly because of the alcohol and partly because of trauma. Alena had a series of dreams that revealed the many layers of her inner turmoil:

A coworker, a Black woman, dies of a ruptured appendix.
I am captured by a group of Hispanics. They attach a
penis to me and put me on tour. I get paid for it.

It was important for Alena and I to discuss the meaning of this troubling dream. This dream told the "secret" but not the specifics of the apparent sexual trauma she had experienced. We explored how the woman in the dream represented Alena and that she had to die. Alena did not feel anything beyond reporting the woman's death. Alena often expressed feelings of self-hate and, especially, hatred of her genitals. She refused to speak more of the dream. Her discomfort was so intense that the subject was dropped temporarily until she could tolerate addressing the symbolic meaning of the attached penis. In quick succession, Alena's dreams revealed the deeply rooted pain of abandonment:

> I am sleeping outside. I am looking through a window.
> I cannot go inside. I am forced to stay outside.

In her family, Alena told me, she felt herself to be an outsider. In her experience, her older brother was the favored child and she had nothing in common with him. Alena felt that she could never earn the esteem that her brother had earned from their parents. While her brother was the "good" child, Alena was seen as quite the opposite: the problem child. Her mother was preoccupied with the younger siblings. Her father was isolated and did not confide in anyone. Nowhere in the family could she find an ally whom she could trust. She spent her whole childhood outside the loop and now, in her adult years, she elected to stay out of the loop, with the exception of keeping in touch with the younger children in the family. One dream after another that Alena revealed was distressing, showing anxiety and agitation:

> I am on my way to pick up a friend for dinner. I am
> wandering around town. I finally find a building. There
> is a war. A bomb has hit the building and people are
> injured. I am trying to pick up someone who is injured
> and get through the mess. I get inside and open the
> door to my friend's office. The room is filled with men,

women and children. There is a man on stage forcing
children to have sex.

Alena wept as she recalled this dream. Words to express her pain
were slow in coming; words that could make one's heart break. She
spoke to me of the experiences of her childhood, trauma she had
never shared with anyone.

As a child, Alena was somewhat of a tomboy and felt quite at
home playing games with the boys in the neighborhood, many of
whom were older than she. She liked athletic games and related more
to the traditional boys' games than girls' games. At the time, she was
of an age that, in the normal scheme of things, she would have been
playing with other girls her age, but there were none in the neighborhood. Her parents made no effort to drive her to the homes of her
girlfriends to share time and play. Her mother was too busy and her
father was preoccupied. Looking back, the whole family was too preoccupied to notice that this child, Alena, was a sad little girl.

The boys in the neighborhood were older and only let her play
if she allowed them to "do things to my body." She was only eight
years old when the gang rapes began. They continued for four years,
getting more bizarre as the years went by. The boys ritualized the
rapes and they paid little attention to her pleas to stop and to let her
go. She was released only after they had completed the rituals, each
boy in his own time, regardless of her curfew. Alena was then left to
go home, alone, bruised and frightened, where yet another punishment awaited her at the hands of her mother, because she had missed
her curfew. She had no place to turn; in her mind, if she told her parents, the punishment would be swift and severe and she would not be
allowed to go out and play. Better to keep the secret. Only when the
boys reached high school age and developed other interests did the
rapes stop. Alena was twelve years old.

It was no wonder that Alena could not speak about the humili-
ating display of her naked body in the first dream. Her third dream
exposed the tender age at which the sexual abuse began and the shame

of having the other boys watch the action. Even though fear of death and abandonment were strong themes in this dream, Alena's heroic self was activated. She was able to get the wounded person out of the building, but there was no help or relief there either, only a shocking scene of children being forced to have sex on a stage exposed to everyone in the room. She felt just as she felt as a child. No one would help!

Alena's anger toward her family and friends knew no bounds as she and I began the process of working through the dreams that exposed the sexual and physical abuse she endured as a child. The rage she had held so tightly finally surfaced. Soon she revealed in our sessions still another dream in which the pent-up anger within her was expressed:

> I am in the basement of my parents' home. I am so angry. I am out of control. I am shooting someone, possibly my brother. He has holes in his head, but he will not die. I laugh at him. Then I am in a hospital with gunshot wounds. I am bleeding. Nurses and doctors are there.

Now her dreams allowed the expression of the rage she felt against herself and her family. In the dream she was with her brother (the favored one) and she used a gun to "put holes in him" and then laughed. We spoke of whether this solved anything, for it was Alena who ended up in the hospital bleeding with gunshot wounds, once more attempting to murder her shameful self. She had no tolerance for her body or its female functions, such as menstruation. She lamented that if she had been born a boy, she would not have all this trouble. "You are going to have to deal with who and what you are," I conveyed to her, "because, in the dream, you did not succeed in completing the act." Alena lay bleeding in a hospital bed, but there was a shift in the pattern. Doctors and nurses were attending to her and she was not left to deal with her wounds alone and unaided. I pointed out to Alena that the fact she was not alone was important, because the dream was already predicting the end of the isolation she had felt for many years.

Alena's waking life was a nightmare. Her friends and partner seemed to be on a nonstop mission to destroy her self-confidence. Their verbal, psychological and emotional abuse was constant. She was blamed, shamed and accused on a daily basis. Furthermore, as the abuse continued, Alena began to drink more alcohol, more often. It was a vicious cycle from which Alena saw no escape. Her opinion of herself was so low and her mood so despondent that she began contemplating suicide to end her suffering. She held to our agreement regarding suicidal thoughts and allowed those thoughts to fade away. Alena did not like losing and she was not going to be a loser by committing suicide. She attempted to be present at her therapy sessions to the best of her ability, but she was quickly losing ground with her addiction. Alena accepted that she was not worthy of anything, but she would not accept that she no longer had control over her addictions. "Psyche never sleeps," I observed. Alena got her wake-up call through a dream:

> Two female friends and I are running from the law in a
> dangerous slum area. There is a coke house there.
> Women I know are inside stoned. I share drugs with
> those women in the house. I am afraid of more coke,
> but I do coke anyway. Then I am running. There is chaos
> and many cars are there.

We talked about the meaning of the dream telling her to run. The question was: run where? Although guilt and shame were major themes throughout Alena's journey into the unconscious, these strong feelings did not serve as a deterrent to her alcohol use. The specter of punishment continuously hung over her like a dark cloud and shortly after this dream, almost as prophesied, Alena was arrested for driving while under the influence.

Ordinarily I assign one task at a time; however, Alena was going to have to multitask. Alena could no longer pretend that she could handle her drinking. On more than one occasion she came to our sessions intoxicated. Her problems at home were getting worse. At this point I felt it was apparent that Alena needed intensive care. When I mentioned admitting herself to a rehabilitation facility I was met with denials and protests that she would lose her job if she were to take time off to rehabilitate. Finally, when all else failed, I advised her that no meaningful therapy could take place in the condition she was in and we would have to stop meeting. I encouraged her to speak confidentially with her employer with the intention of admitting herself to a hospital. She was reluctant but, with my assurance that she could resume therapy, she agreed to talk with her employer. Without hesitation her employer granted Alena a leave of absence on the basis of medical need.

Alena's first attempt to arrange for her admission was met with complications. In fact, she had no health insurance coverage for this type of treatment. Fortunately there were funds available in the company's healthcare system for employees who battled addictions and wanted to enter into an intensive treatment program. The human resources director was knowledgeable about where Alena could gain access to the funds. When the funds were made available to her, she admitted herself to a rehabilitation hospital with the blessings of her employer and coworkers and the hope for her full recovery.

Built into the treatment program she entered was family therapy. Family members were invited to attend the meetings. Alena's mother and brother attended, but her father refused. Alena felt rejected and angered by his lack of support but even in spite of this obvious disappointment she completed the program. When she graduated into an aftercare partial program, she returned to therapy with me, ready and willing to engage in the process of change.

Now Alena was ready to fill in the spaces from childhood through adolescence and discuss them so she could move on. In our sessions, Alena recalled feeling unsettled and searching for a sense of belonging wherever she could find it. She found it easier to fit in with the students who were experimenting with drugs, alcohol and sex. By the age of twelve, Alena began to use drugs and alcohol to fit in with the group. Any group and any substance would do to deaden her pain. She became sexually active at an early age, always with residual self-hate. Alena described those years as being drugged and out of control. She lived in a fog and cared little about herself. She barely managed her schoolwork even though she previously had excellent grades all through her elementary and secondary education.

Alena's performance in school began deteriorating. Recognizing Alena's potential and her apparent distress, her teachers intervened, suggesting to her parents that Alena might benefit from seeing a professional counselor to help improve her school performance. She had a few sessions with the school psychologist; however, her parents did not see the value in continuing the process of therapy beyond these few sessions and terminated her relationship with her counselor. Once again, Alena was left to her own devices to try to fit into a world that was confusing and painful.

Alena graduated with her class and entered a university. She earned a bachelor's degree in computer science despite partying, drinking and using any drug she had access to at any opportunity made available to her.

Alena entered into a relationship with her current partner at about age twenty. She had always been faithful to the relationship. At the time Alena began her therapy, both she and her partner were attracted to other people. These events resulted in the awakening of jealousy, insecurity and anger on both sides, resulting in physical fights and emotional and psychological abuse, which was finally coming to an end. Alena and her companion chose to part company but Alena continued to struggle with her attraction to her former partner, creating a situation in which she was trapped by her yearning for belongingness. There was a serious threat of relapse.

Her relationship conditions were so toxic that there was no other alternative but to move on to the next task that Alena needed to master:

separate from her partner and all of her former friends. She had to agree to be lonely. Accepting loneliness is much easier if it is voluntary. Alena confided she was terrified at the thought of being alone and abandoned. "Abandoned?" I questioned her. I discussed with her that this was a voluntary, logical decision for health reasons. "When one makes a decision to separate from any relationship, toxic or nontoxic, one *agrees* to be lonely," I conveyed.

Alena knew that she could not tolerate complete and total aloneness, so she made her way to the local animal shelter where she found Henri, a mixed breed puppy that was patiently waiting for a loving home. It was love at first sight. Henri would prove himself to be the one who would travel the hazardous journey to wellness with her, no matter what that journey would require of him.

Despite the comfort of having Henri with her, Alena's anxiety levels increased to dramatic proportions. Suicidal thoughts were once again emerging. Alena attempted to dismiss these thoughts by physically exercising to the maximum limit of her capacity, creating yet another problem. Her injured foot, which had previously been broken, began to respond with incredible pain that forced Alena to address her activity level. She began her search for the right doctor, the right cure or anything to help with the excruciating pain she was experiencing. It was as though she was addicted to exercise as well as to alcohol. She *had* to exercise as if her life depended on it. She felt trapped in a body that would not respond to her commands anymore. The pain was so intense that it also affected her leg and extended up to her hip.

She felt disconnected from everything. Her self-esteem was at an all-time low. She told me she felt herself to be a "nothing." Alena's resolve to stay the course with her sobriety program was quickly losing ground and she began to binge. Her judgment was poor. Driving her car while intoxicated caught the attention of the police. She failed a sobriety test and was given a citation with a sixty-day suspension from driving. This setback almost put her over the edge. Her already fragile ego could hardly grasp the enormity of the events that were occurring. I was finding that on some level Alena knew she was in a hellish place. However, she needed to work her way out of it before her life would improve in any significant way. Alena's new dreams concerned her current troubles:

> I am in a small town shopping. It is a busy store, people going in and out. I am afraid to buy the clothes. I go back and forth with the clothes. A man tells me that I am going with him. He forcibly takes me. There are several women around him and they follow his orders. They take me to a primitive camp setting. I have to be naked. I am trying to get away. People are watching me. He picks me to have sex with him, but I fight and struggle with him. People are following him. He has an erect penis in a bag and is carrying it. Then we are in a dirty, filthy house and I am also dirty and doing drugs, animal-like. I am lying in feces. Someone comes and carries me out and puts me in a car.

We discussed how this dream informed her that much of the gains she had made in the hospital had been lost. Alena associated the shopping for clothes with the action of taking off the old and putting on the new. But what is the old? What is the new? There was more than alcohol in the old. There was the ability to tolerate a tremendous amount of punishment. She did not yet know the "new," even though she had been through rehabilitation and had been taught the many ways of combating the need for drink and drugs. Alena had not yet integrated this knowledge and had relapsed several times. (This is not unusual in the struggle to gain mastery over an addiction.) Therefore, it was possible that she was not ready yet for the "new."

As I interpreted it, in this dream she dallied too long and she was punished once again; this time, with the threat of rape. Once more, the traumatic experience of the ultimate "punishment" (rape) entered the dream world and, as in her actual experience of the rapes, she found herself to be in a state of complete and utter humiliation: "I have to be naked." It was no wonder that her opinion of herself was so low. Clearly, Alena had not yet developed enough ego strength to be less vulnerable and more self-protective. This dream also spoke to the symptoms of post-traumatic stress disorder: the early experience of trauma that kept emerging again and again. The rapist in the dream had an erect penis at the ready, just as the boys from Alena's childhood were always at the ready. Alena found that in this dirty place with the dirty people, she was reduced to primitive, feral behavior: "I am also dirty and doing drugs, animal-like. I am lying in feces." It was only when she had gotten as low as she could get (hit the bottom) that there was, once again, redemption: "Someone comes and carries me out and puts me in a car." Putting on the "new" was still a future goal for Alena.

It was important that Alena came to realize that so long as she lived an emotional existence, out of control, her dreams of brutal men would continue to haunt her. "Remember," I reiterated to her, "psyche demands balance! Balance is putting together the coolness of logic and reason with the emotional intensity of feeling; creating a wide range of options for how to attend to any situation."

Some situations call for cool logic, such as decisions at work, and others call for passionate responses, such as fear, joy or anger. Alena had been bingeing on more than alcohol. She binged on exercise and emotional outbursts. That was a lot of bingeing and her body protested the abuse she was imposing on it. Her doctors warned her of the real possibility of irreversible damage if she did not cease the grueling routine she had established for herself. Finally, Alena could no longer deny that she had reached her limit of tolerance for pain and she refocused her efforts on conquering her alcohol addiction.

Alena began in earnest to enter into the world of sobriety. She had stopped using drugs but had continued to use alcohol to excess from time to time. In keeping with her new resolution, she began attending Alcoholics Anonymous meetings on a daily basis and made friends with her peers in the program, but despite her best efforts, she continued to relapse and then stopped attending. The demon, alcohol, does not give up easily. She could not get away, not even in her dreams. She shared a recent one with me and we discussed its meaning:

> I am in a house, my own house. My partner, her lover and Henri are there. She is taking over. I start to throw fruit at her. There is a large spider-like bug that keeps getting on my hand. I am desperate and irritable. The women grab me and put me into a fire truck or ambulance. Then I am trying to get into a house to rescue someone: a man and a woman. He killed his wife and himself. He is my peer at work. But I can do nothing; I keep meeting detours. All the swimming pools are closed. Subways are out of control, smashing through buildings. This is a roller coaster type ride. I am holding on! We are going straight up and down the track and then sliding backwards. I am crying for help, but no one answers my call. Then I am watching a parade. My cousin Harry is drunk. I am jealous that he can drink, so I drink too. The women join me. I see my cousin Trudy with a long leg brace, cheerleading in the parade.

It was important that our sessions focused on the present. The entire trauma that Alena was experiencing in her waking life was in the dream: her preoccupation with alcohol, her rage against her "friends," the need to kill and be killed at one level and to be the rescuer at another level, the terrible descent into addiction and the crippling of her ability to enjoy her body without pain. Alena and I noted that the "crippling" did not affect Cousin Trudy, a female about Alena's age who symbolized her own self in the dream. Trudy was marching on, cheerleading, brace and all! Trudy was the other side of the coin:

the healthy, happy young woman who embodied the real soul and spirit of Alena.

After this dream our sessions intensified. On some level Alena began to realize her potential and she rose to the occasion. Alena launched a new effort to maintain sobriety. She began once more to attend Alcoholics Anonymous and Narcotics Anonymous meetings on a regular basis and humbly identified herself as an addict and an alcoholic. This was very difficult for Alena, who often maintained that she was not *really* an alcoholic or an addict. Eventually, invested in the programs, she proceeded to do the necessary work to come to terms with her addictions and made yet another effort to establish a lifestyle of sobriety. I reassured her, "That's what it takes: try, try again and, once again, try."

With Alena's increased and earnest efforts to gain and maintain sobriety, her alcoholic dreams increased dramatically. The themes of these dreams were abandonment and threats of punishment of the worst kind. Themes of rape and torture were represented in graphic detail. One proved to be especially insightful:

> I am in a camp workshop waiting in line to shower. I step into open showers. There is no privacy. There are women everywhere. I undress in front of a large window. There are people outside. A police officer in a car rides by, stops to look at me and goes on by. After I shower, the policeman bursts into the room to arrest me for indecent exposure. I call him an obscene name. I run and two female police officers chase me. I stop. They rough me up and accuse me and threaten to incarcerate me for a year. I fight back with them but they tie me down on a stretcher, telling me that I will be locked up with other addicts. I cry. I plead. I beg them not to take me. I tell them that I will starve myself. Several of the women tell me that this will be good for me. I am curled up in a fetal position.

Our session continued as I explored with Alena that much had to be done to help her to accept what had happened, integrate it into all of her life experiences and allow for the transformed Alena to emerge from the darkness of her past. She vowed that she would not give up until the goal was realized. Psyche was helping her to keep focused on the task at hand.

Another dream conveyed that Alena was making progress:

I am in a camp. Many people are there. It is a primitive, commune-type tent. There is a large dog in front of the tent, mutilated. His organs are exposed. Everyone is examining the dog. I am not, because I am crying for the dog. I enter the big tent. Rituals, ceremonies and parties are going on. Then a woman takes all the women in the area to telephone poles with big baskets on them. We have to climb up and sit in the basket on the pole. At first, I will not go, but I am eventually forced to go. I am frozen. Then I am screaming. The woman will not let others help. I make it to the top, but I am afraid to come back down.

The tide was turning, I could see, slowly but surely. This dream revolved around rites of passage, which originated in ancient times. "Rites of passage always mean struggle and tasks that must be mastered before one can go on to the next step in psychological development," I explained to her. Alena was entering a primitive, ritualistic ceremony where mutilation of animals appeared to be part of the process (the dog's organs were exposed). In tribal societies, sacrificing animals to the gods is a part of the ritual. Alena was joining in an ancient and time-honored ritual. It was as though Alena was given a sign that the ceremony she was about to engage in would make her feel like her very organs were being torn out of her body. Even though Alena identified with the pain of the dog and wept for him, she did not "examine" him as the others were in the process of doing but instead she elected to go into the "big tent" to submit to the task.

The ceremony she was to take part in was directed by a woman. Furthermore, all the women had to participate in the ceremony, whether they wanted to do so or not. The goal appeared to be "getting to the top." Who would quarrel with such a goal? Even though Alena was screaming in terror, the woman in authority did not permit others to help. Alena had to make it to the top herself, however terrifying the journey. Getting to the top was one task which Alena had to complete; her other task was being brave enough to come back down. Alena did make it to the top. Since the dream ended at this point, we did not know how Alena negotiated the journey back down.

Getting back down can be traumatic. As Alena began to gain some mastery over her addiction, she became more irritable and angry. When one is in withdrawal, emotions can be very unpredictable. Alena began to focus on her past experiences of rape, especially on her vaginal area. She hated her sexual organs! Her grief was so intense, she revealed to me, that she screamed and cried and grieved to the point that she behaved as a very young, wounded child, crawling about on the floor and eventually ending up in the fetal position. As we continued to explore her feelings I explained that since she elected to no longer anesthetize herself with alcohol and drugs to ward off the horrific memories she had safely hidden for years, she was now subject to a serious reaction to the abuses she had experienced all through her young life. Henri, her dog, was not frightened by this grievous demonstration of emotional pain. He patiently lay beside her and eventually they both slept, sometimes under a table and sometimes Alena made her way to her bed. This gripping grief reaction lasted several months. No effort was made to intervene except for support. Alena had to feel the pain and allow the poisons to work their way out. There was no danger of suicide. She was not going to leave Henri to be sent back to the shelter.

During this hellish time, Alena resolved not to give up and drew many illustrations of her hated vagina in an effort to bring out the rage to a point where she could deal with it consciously. To help externalize the grief process, I asked her to try to draw the tragic child who crawled on the floor and wept. She drew a child she described as "one who cries black tears." Her response to this child was hatred. Alena referred to her as a "stupid, dirty, little kid." I found nothing surprising about this. The "stupid, dirty, little kid" was the image of herself Alena always had experienced since she was eight years old.

With the extreme reaction to the child in her dream and the acute worsening of an already serious situation, Alena's layers of wounds were slowly unfolding into consciousness. I analyzed that the child who cried black tears was Alena regressed to a very young age, unimaginably abandoned and alone. She recognized the extent of the trauma she experienced, but recognizing and accepting are two very different things. Unless she accepted that bad things happen to good people, so to speak, she could go no further in her goal of getting to the top. We discussed that getting to the top meant using her experience to bring forth a "new" Alena. It also meant accepting the things she could not change and integrating them into her whole life experience instead of holding them apart, hoping that they would set her free. "Accepting does not mean diminishing the experience," I advised Alena. "It means that we accept what we cannot change and continue on to the future. To dwell in it is to be at a standstill. Life never seems to get better."

Although courageous and willing to take an active role in her own healing process, Alena's dreams continued to reflect the traumatic events of her life. I believe psyche was helping her to cleanse herself of the pain so she could go forward into life, healed and hopeful for her future. Alena contributed a new dream:

> I am at my elementary school gathering. There are men and women there. We are being controlled by leaders. We have to do a circle dance. I am outside the circle. I refuse to participate. A man grabs me by my arm and

drags me into the circle. He has a very tight hold on me.
I am with several addicts. My mother is there with my
aunt, watching me and them. I am a captive of my
mother. Large bags of cocaine are brought in and put in
front of me. I am confused. Two women from high
school are there. They had accepted me in school and
gave me booze and drugs. They want to take me to a
party. I tell them I am in recovery. They tell me that they
can understand why. Now, I am outside. My partner and
her friend are there. I can sense intense sexual energy.

I asked myself, *What have we here?* Alena felt herself to be a victim
in the dream. Something very different was going on. The mother and
man *thought* they were in charge. The group banded together to convince Alena to "dance the dance" with drugs and booze. Alena
declined and then she was almost magically transported away: "I am
outside." What was outside was yet another reality she had to face:
loss of her partner and friend. She did not break down, only took note
that they were in an intimate relationship.

Sexuality, particularly her own sexual nature, was repulsive to
her. When psychological problems are overwhelming and not
resolved, the body can and does bear the burden. Her repulsion was
soon made evident by the physical symptoms she developed in
response to the sexual trauma. Inexplicably, her menses stopped. She
did not menstruate for many months. Doctors could find nothing
physically wrong to explain the phenomenon. It was as though Alena
could not bear to own her feminine self and in expending so much
energy in an effort to destroy it, her body decided to cooperate with
her. She began to question her attraction to women. She was not sure
whether this attraction was a reaction to the early experiences of rape
or a genuine predisposition to homosexuality. However, Alena's fear
and distrust of men would not stop. These strong emotions were
reflected in her next dreams:

I am at a seminar. There is a tall, athletic man there. He was sent by a Higher Power, a spiritual being. I sense negativity, evil. He is trying to get me to go with him; in fact, he insists that I go with him. He is touching me. Others are watching. I am frightened. He has magical powers. The others become frantic and climb up a wooden sculpture. The Power is pulling it down. I am almost unconscious and only sort of aware of what is going on. The event ends. He picks me up and carries me off.

In the second dream, I am at a party with my partner. The party is on a boat. We are taking a trip somewhere. Our old party friends are there. I am nervous. There are beautiful women at the party. I am feeling inferior. My partner and I leave the party. We are on the run in a river boat. She is steering. We keep running into small boats with people in them. They capsize. People begin to chase us. Now we are on a train. A man approaches us and offers us a place to stay. He takes us to a large house on a hill. He seems to be okay, but I feel that he has an evil side. We go with him to a huge mansion. I feel it is haunted. I am afraid of it, but my companion wants to stay. The man follows us everywhere. He is vigilant and controlling. I feel that he gets women to this house and controls them mentally, emotionally and sexually. He is dangerous like the others in my life. He proceeds to torture me mentally and sexually. I call for my partner. There is no response. One day he seems disoriented. I beat him unconscious or dead. I put him in a large pool of water and let him sink. I feel sorry for him and want to save him.

I helped Alena interpret the theme of both these dreams: women were helpless and men controlled everything. They were so gifted that they had the powers of God (the Higher Power), carried her off and even pulled the wooden structure down with all the women hanging on for dear life. There was also the replay of the trauma, but the action was new and different on Alena's part. She took action; she planned. When the time was right, she escaped after she beat her attacker unconscious or dead. Unless she took action, she would be doomed to be the eternal victim. This time she rescued herself through logically planning and executing her plan. Even so, she felt sorry for this man and wanted to save him. Rightly so: he was her companion, her inner male in the unconscious and he could turn helpful if she thought and planned before reacting to everything and taking refuge in the victim's role. In the final analysis, she was her own rescuer. A dream of mastery was the first step toward true mastery of her destiny:

> I am a participant with other men and women at a
> training seminar. We are assigned the task of climbing
> up rocks. I am left alone with the training instructor. He
> is an older man who is very aggressive with the
> students. He is observing me closely. I am paranoid and
> feel unsafe with him. I continue to be in his presence. I
> am alone. He corners me in a small room and rapes me.
> He hurts me. He is very strong and behaving like an
> animal. I am overpowered and he rapes me many times.
> I go numb and let him do this. I dissociate. I just lay
> there. He tells me that I am his and whenever he wants
> me, I will come to him.

Alena's still frequent and unrelenting dreams of being punished, raped and abused had two elements she and I considered. One was the trauma of rape and abuse yet to be resolved in the psyche and the other was the element of the inner male. "He brings to the female dreamer the ability to be logical and problem solving," I reminded Alena. "When a woman is in an emotional state and is neglecting these functions, he is said to be neglected and becomes the tormentor alongside the rapists and a mother figure. It is my strong belief that to be whole, we need all functions. If our destiny is to be something more than we are then we can expect torment until we make the decision to change the unhealthy situation."

After this dream Alena was so frightened of being overpowered that she seemed to take a renewed interest in her attendance at the Alcoholics and Narcotics Anonymous meetings and experienced fewer relapses due to the strong support system she had built up within the two groups. Alena's menses had not yet started, but several months later she developed symptoms of premenstrual cramping. She suffered severe, debilitating pain each month. The pain was so intense that, on several occasions, she was forced to seek emergency care at a hospital. She had menstrual symptoms but no sign of blood. The doctors determined that the cause was not physical. Alena's body had picked up the burden and it did not like it at all. As she lay in the emergency room of her local hospital with waves of pain enveloping her body, she experienced a sudden pain so intense that it could be equated to giving birth. I asked her to describe the experience. She recalled feeling a burning, piercing sensation in her vagina as if a huge Serpent was entering her vaginal cavity. The Serpent swiftly and mercilessly bit her. She could not stop screaming and had to be sedated. The image that she later drew of the experience was startling. The Serpent was blood red and ferocious. There would be no mercy here! Alena's totem had arrived. Change was now inevitable. To refuse the task was to get more of the same.

Oftentimes, an animal spirit guide will make its appearance when a dreamer is reluctant to move on with her life. We all have a destiny and if one dallies and refuses to seek the way to fulfilling that destiny, the first appearance of the totem, in this case the Serpent, will be painful, piercing, biting and merciless. In the tradition of totem medicine, the Serpent is the totem that calls for transformation and renewal. Alena was now being offered Serpent medicine to begin her journey into new beginnings. Soon after the experience of the Serpent bite, she began to bring forth little trickles of blood. Nothing major yet, but it appeared that she was beginning to let go of her rage against herself.

Alena's Nasty, Mean Serpent

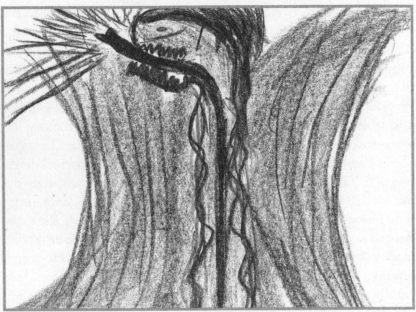

Even so, Alena did not see that this painful experience of the Serpent could signify anything but more of the same: suffering. Although patience was difficult for Alena, she agreed to continue with the therapy work in progress in spite of her doubts that this mean-spirited Serpent could ever evolve into anything positive. In fact, I soon discovered Alena had been thinking about change and what change would mean to her future security. She had not yet discussed this with me, because she did not see that anything good could or would happen in her life. But now she began to share with me a wish she had of devoting more time to her healing professions.

At this point Alena shared with me that she was finding little satisfaction in her work as a computer analyst and longed to put more time and effort into her real love: using her hands in the Reiki tradition to promote health and well-being in her clients. After many discussions, a strategy to transition from full-time computer analyst to part-time was in place. This showed she was spending time thinking and planning. Alena bravely approached her supervisor and was granted her request to work on a reduced hourly basis. This meant less predictable income; however, despite her anxiety, she forged ahead with her plans to build her Reiki practice.

Alena was not content to concentrate on the Reiki practice alone, knowing full well that she would have idle time on her hands. She decided to forge ahead to earn certification as a dietician. Her logic was sound. She was *thinking* through her plans and the possible outcomes. If she were certified as a dietician, she could utilize her knowledge of healing with proper nutrition along with the usual and customary nutritional suggestions to promote healing at an advanced level, such as treating people who suffer with diabetes. Equally important, with certification Alena could work in partnership with other healthcare professionals and take the appropriate steps to become a provider of services for insurance companies. Thus her income would become more stable.

This was not going to be an easy task to accomplish, since Alena would be relying on her savings to pay for further education. The program to which she chose to apply was some distance away from her home and this placed extra pressure on her to keep her vehicle in good condition and to be ever more vigilant of her desire for drugs and alcohol, not to mention the added cost of travel. There was much to think about. "Could this really happen?" she asked me. She and I decided to take a vote. Our choice was unanimous: *yes!* We agreed she was to continue with Alcoholics Anonymous and Narcotics Anonymous and keep regular therapy hours, so as not to defer the task of healing. This was a tall order but necessary for Alena's psychological development.

Alena maintained sobriety with occasional relapses. Overall, her attendance to her work and school requirements was above average. As she progressed, her menstrual periods stabilized, but she continued to have very painful cramping. Her drawings were evolving and becoming lighter. Even though they continued to reflect the multiple traumatizing events of her life, they were not as fierce as before.

Her sexuality and the trauma surrounding it was an ever-present theme in her drawings. She felt "boxed in" and recognized how reluctant she was to even *think* of a meaningful sexual encounter. The only way she could accept males as friends was to imagine them to be castrated and, therefore, harmless. Fortunately, this attitude toward men changed for the better over time. These were the days when we discussed Alena's sexual preference in earnest. It is an understandable phenomenon that a sexually abused female child could develop an intense distrust of and aversion to males. It is also understandable that even the thought of a male sexual organ penetrating the vagina could provoke a negative reaction, but what of the everyday activities that necessarily include males? Alena was estranged from her former partner. She was essentially without a social relationship with either man or woman. While she cherished and appreciated the friendship of others in the support groups, they could not meet her needs for fun and playtime after a long week's work.

During this period, Alena was beginning to attract the attention of males other than her long-term, platonic male relationships. Her attraction to one man actually went beyond friendship, suggesting that Alena was possibly bisexual and, as such, could choose the way she wished to live in the world. This was not an easy task. Alena's dreams continued to torment her with punishment and shame. In her dreams, men and women alike made the most of the opportunity to inflict pain on her:

> My dog and I are running errands. We are in a plaza.
> Around the corner there are two women and a dog.
> They are talking about dogs. My dog starts to bark and

snarl in an effort to protect me. Then I am alone outside in the dark. There is chaos everywhere. There is a group of women who are in recovery. They are both gay and straight. They are listening to a friend play the piano. Then, without warning, a group of women back up in a car, driving erratically. They run over a massage table. I try to run away. Someone is running after me. They catch me and beat me. Everyone in the plaza is observing this. Then a riot breaks out. Everyone is fighting. Someone takes me in the back to a cabin. Others are lurking about. One man recognizes me. He starts to chase me. Another man intercedes and uses kung fu to fight him off. I grab my attacker's crotch and squeeze really hard. Women are cheering me on. I want to kill him! A psychologist stops the fight. The women want to take me to jail.

As in Alena's life experience, it is my firm conviction that there is no safe route to negotiate through or around the plaza of life without harm or the threat of harm. In Alena's dream, neither the men nor the women could be relied upon to help when she was attacked. Once again, as in her previous dreams, Alena fought back and was the victor. There was a new twist in this dream: a psychologist stopped the fight.

I felt "stops the fight" seemed to be a good place to start discussing the message contained in the dream. Surely, to continue the fight would only lead to more of the same. In exploring the idea of stopping the fight, family was foremost on the agenda of tasks that needed to be addressed. After much thought and discussion Alena agreed to allow her parents to come to a family therapy session. Both her mother and father attended the meeting. Alena bravely shared the events of her childhood with her parents. These revelations moved her parents to tears and Alena could not hold back her own. At last she allowed herself to acknowledge that her parents loved her!

Nonetheless, she could not bring herself to reconnect further with them in a meaningful way just yet.

Even so, this event proved to be a vitally important turning point in Alena's life. Images of the hated vagina slowly began to take on a new character. She was more accepting of her womanly self and actually seemed to be proud that her menses had started and her body was functioning as it should. The images of her body were becoming healing in nature; so much so that the original images seemed as if they were from a distant time. Her relationship to her Serpent totem was also changing. The images that were emerging in her consciousness were of being surrounded by gentle serpents, protecting her from harm.

Even as Alena held steadfast to her goals, she had little confidence that she would be able to meet them. She was afraid to hope that her life could possibly turn around permanently. She was always waiting for the disaster that she was sure was just around the corner. During this period her dreams reflected this fear she had known for most of her life:

> I am with a group of women in the country. There is
> some type of gathering in this large old house. We will
> repair, clean and refurbish it to make it livable. My old
> roommate is there. There is a large stairwell with a large
> wall supporting one side of it. It comes crashing down on
> me and the other women. I am underneath the debris.

I analyzed that Alena's dream spoke of comfort in the presence of women as opposed to men as long as her mother was not involved. She was able to work in community with women to "repair, clean and refurbish" the country house; however, it was as if her worst fears were realized in this dream: the wall came crashing down and pinned her to the ground. It was clear to me that her self-confidence was very fragile and she continued to be apprehensive in all areas of her life. This fragility was reflected mainly in her relationships with men. She was unable to reach a level of comfort in her interactions with them, even though she was social and friendly. She liked them and enjoyed their company, but she was not comfortable with intimacy at any level, even as she craved the closeness that they offered.

It did not help much that Alena was attracting very needy men who appeared to be unable to interact with her on an adult level. She found herself becoming angrier with them and continued to repress her sexual feelings. The antidote for Alena was exercising, studying and working very hard to suppress her desire for intimacy. Under this grueling regimen, Alena was able to stabilize and become somewhat philosophical about male/female relationships. At this stage, Alena elected to confine herself to heterosexual relationships and no longer attempted to contact her former roommate or any other potential female partners.

Physically, she was experiencing intense pain; psychologically, she became focused on career change. After many failed attempts to salvage her current heterosexual relationship, including attending couples therapy, Alena terminated her relationship with the man she had been seeing and concentrated more on the friends that she was making in her training program as she continued forward with her studies in nutrition. In this program she was exposed to healthy food, tai chi, yoga and lectures from well-known professionals. Social activities were part of the program and offered an antidote to the intensity of the courses. She was committed to attaining the greatest available benefit for herself and her future. Her dreams began to reflect her attention to herself and the healing that was now occurring in a most beautiful way:

> I am in my childhood neighborhood. There is chaos everywhere; lots of people and activities. I sense danger. There is a little girl wandering around, lost, upset and crying. There is a group of people in my parents' basement. They bring the little girl to me. I take her and console her.

At last, Alena was able to take ownership of her wounded child-self and care for the little girl. Alena described seeing a golden light surrounding the child's head, suggesting the dawning of a new day, a sign of lightness and energy and the new beginnings that were already apparent in her waking life.

I believe old learning is never, ever lost. It can emerge anytime, given the right trigger. Alena experienced an extended period of grief following her disappointment with the failure of her latest attempt at a romantic relationship. This event evoked once again the horror of rape. Flashbacks began to emerge. She recalled more of the details, such as the ages of the boys, which she placed at around age fifteen when she was eight years old. Alena agonized over the memory of the haunted eight-year old she once was. Her description of the child was a poignant tribute to her innocence.

At this stage, even though Alena was in a grievous state, she was wavering between a strong sense of purpose with regard to her ambitions and incredible vulnerability in her interpersonal relationships. The level of physical pain Alena was experiencing increased dramatically after the breakup of her relationship. She began to realize that she had been an anchor for others but those same people who needed her could not provide support in return. The very thing she dreaded came to pass under the stress of the situation: She suffered a relapse! After fifteen months in recovery, Alena began to abuse alcohol again, as she usually did when life became impossible for her to manage.

The ego of the child who has not been nurtured and protected is fragile indeed. Fortunately, at this stage of Alena's therapy, setbacks were often of short duration before the uphill climb began anew. The beauty of gains realized before a setback is that they are usually permanent gains and not easily destroyed, so nothing is ever lost.

Alena quickly recovered, increased her attendance at AA meetings, made the necessary adjustments and picked up where she left off. Fortunately, her schoolwork did not suffer, but she was sad and her appearance betrayed her feelings. She felt disconnected from her body and unsure of herself with regard to problem solving. As luck would have it, her studies were more demanding and exacting than she could ever imagine. This was a good thing for Alena, because, above all, her goals and ambitions were solid. She threw herself into her work despite her grief and self-blame. Eventually, her school routine became prominent in her daily life.

Throughout the course of our therapy together, Alena recovered memories of rape not previously available to her and these times were trying for her. However, as she worked through and accepted her experiences, I saw healing images emerge in her drawings and dreams. The Serpent was prominent in some of the drawings as a healing, protective creature. Color, form and light slowly emerged, in contrast to the darkness and chaos of earlier dreams. Serpent totem visited her again in her dreams:

> I am sitting in the front seat of a car. All of a sudden, a large snake bites me on the right side of my neck. Then she bites me a second time on my finger. The snake bites hurt, but it is not a poisonous snake.

Alena recognized that to be faced with change and transformation was a painful process. She recalled the nasty, mean Serpent that invaded her body and marveled at the transformation of the nature of the Serpent when she experienced its bite in this latest dream. She recognized that growth was inevitable but that it took perseverance and fortitude to be mindful of and respond to the call of the soul, to strive for balance and to be all that she could be. The darkness that permeated earlier dreams was now diminished in importance, giving way to her acceptance of divine, healing Serpent medicine. In her accompanying drawing, Alena's hands enjoined the Serpent in peace and love. The Serpent appeared to grow out of the depths of the earth, arising from the acorn to full blossom surrounded by colorful wings. This is not an individually generated dream image from the dreamer's personal experience. It is a universal dream image arising from the deepest layers of the unconscious mind and belongs not only to Alena, but to all of humankind.

Alena's Healing Serpent Over Me

Herein we see the full power of the spiritual, awe-inspiring, sacred symbol of the totem. The image and experience of the divine totem show what therapy can expect to achieve when it goes into the deep layers of the mind by way of dreams. Alena was healing. The healing process was reflected in Alena's images, her change in attitude and her drawings. At this juncture, she composed a poem expressing her acceptance of her life experience:

Alena's Poem

My ears of my heart hear its own pounding.
The throb of life with a deep current of water
Flowing through the throbs.
Running, running, running to leap from the cliff.
Leaving my held-fast anchor,
Trusting that my hang glider will guide me
Through the winds.
The pockets of new winds catch my wings
As I soar over valleys, rivers, cliffs and ledges.
Where will these winds take me next?
What new spaces will I glide into?
What new sounds, vibrations, visions will I receive?
Blow into the familiar dark.
Downward plunge, tumbling, hurdling, descending
Into the darkness.
I find myself in an ancient village,
Lurking around the corners of the narrow, uneven cobblestones.
Each cobblestone engraved with unspoken tales and truths.
As I leave the village of Wisdom, I find
The heavy stones filled with unspoken truths
Piled high upon my back.
Heavy, oh! So heavy!
I pull myself up the mountain to fly once again
And release my stones of truth to the winds.

Over time, I found positive changes in Alena's attitude. Her lifestyle appeared to be more stable and therefore lent itself to her moving forward.

Alena's next task was to reconnect with her family on a meaningful level. Even though some healing had occurred in the family therapy session, Alena had not followed through with actively pursuing a truly loving and trusting relationship with her parents. Trust had not yet been realized. Alena persevered and, at the time most suitable for her, she made her feelings known to her mother. To her surprise, her mother was very receptive to her overtures. In a surprisingly short time, she and Alena developed a close and loving relationship. Alena began to understand the pressures that her mother must have experienced with two challenged children and little emotional support from her father.

Sadly, Alena could not connect with her father in the same way. He remained distant and isolated from her and the family in general. Then the family was blessed with a grandchild. Alena was now Aunt Alena. Her face revealed her joy and pride in this newest addition to her life. She boldly and bravely accepted her role and was even able to give advice to the new parents based on her graduate work in nutrition and her knowledge of Reiki. To her surprise, they respected her advice and followed through with her suggestions. The birth of the child served yet a greater purpose. Alena was now able to connect with her older brother in a way she had never realized in the past and she was able to witness her father's joy in the acceptance of his role as grandfather. Alena quickly bonded to the child and found, in the tiny miracle she held so tenderly, the capacity to love unconditionally with no reservations or need to suppress her feelings.

Alena persevered, completed her graduate programs and busied herself with establishing a practice of her own in nutrition and Reiki. She was successful working with other professionals and acquired a stable referral base. Other healthcare providers began to seek her out and eventually Alena joined a professional group whose focus was on women's issues. Their reputation grew and the practice expanded to lecturing and providing workshops for women in addition to providing services in counseling and healing using the principles of mind-body techniques. Alena had found purpose in life. She was able to embrace life to the fullest.

Having reached her goals, our therapeutic partnership was now coming to an end. The imagery for this experience was the Serpent in its divine form: the Serpent as healer, the herald of change, of new beginnings, of wisdom and knowledge. Alena understood that totem medicine knows no ethnic, racial or cultural boundaries. Totem medicine binds us together as one. Alena's journey toward wellness and personal empowerment was well on its way. She was now developing and maintaining her own business and becoming self-sufficient. She had formed many true and meaningful relationships with women who, like herself, were dedicated to helping other women travel the perilous road toward personal empowerment. She had a well-balanced social life that included men and women, a thriving health practice and a meaningful and fulfilling relationship with her family. Alena said to me at one of our last sessions, "I am truly blessed."

In Alena's Words:

When I walked into Dr. Strick's office at the age of twenty-nine, I was beaten down by life and felt shattered into pieces. The wounds of my internal world were bleeding heavily and oozing poison throughout my body and psyche. I was in the death grips of addiction and unresolved childhood trauma (sexual abuse). I wanted to die. I was dying and Spirit led me to therapy that day. Thus, I began my soul healing and took my first of many steps back toward life. The Snake had yet to appear. She began to move slightly and uncoil.

Thousands of painful steps toward life, healing and integration followed that day in February. Somehow I was able to desperately hold on to the survivor part of me and fight for my life. My life and self were reduced to ashes and decay; however, my life force was smoldering underneath the dark decay. The smoldering light burned deep in my pelvis and vagina, embedded in a black hole of terror, hopelessness and self-hate.

My wounded, traumatized and terrified child-self was lost in the black hole, smothered by the heavy pile of decay and ash. She was screaming in despair and horror. The time had arrived for me to go down into the hole to save her, to bring her back to life and up into the light. I needed to take this shamanic journey into the dark hole of horrifying pain and despair and transform the raging self-destructive forces within my soma and psyche.

A Snake began to emerge from my unconscious and from the ashes in my pelvis through dreams, artwork and bodywork. She became a guide and ally in my journey, in my life/death cycle of transformation. She lay tightly coiled and asleep beneath the pile of decay and ash. I needed her power, creativity and wisdom to bring my wounded child back to life and to put the shattered pieces of myself back together.

The beginning of this sacred journey was eruptive, chaotic and messy. As the Snake began to uncoil, my tightly held-in energy and emotion began to dismantle the ancient structures of my soma and psyche. She guided me to a landmine. The bomb exploded in my pelvis. The landmines were everywhere, close to the surface, waiting to be stepped on. There was shrapnel, debris, blood and destruction all over the place. I was a bloody mess for everyone to see. I could not move, like the first time that I was raped as a little girl. My wounded child was fighting for her life and the Snake's forces were showing up for the fight.

As I pieced myself back together, the Snake consistently presented herself to guide me up from the black hole. Throughout my healing, she spoke often to me.

Snake: "I see your pieces. I see your wholeness and I am here to help you weave your pieces into a more full wholeness. The weaving of your pieces into the wholeness of your soul is beautiful, hopeful and alive with sorrow and joy. Alena, see your pieces; embrace your journey into wholeness."

Snake: "I am uncoiling from a seed deep in your underground, deep within your pelvis. I am rising with much power, grace and life force. Touch your creativity and wisdom that moves through your heart and out of your throat. I am guiding your sacred feminine and strong masculine into a passionate union. You need your courage."

Snake: "I am hissing from the murky depths of your soul. Listen to me, Alena; come and feed me. I need you to feed me. My forces are erupting and hold much power. I am unfolding from a very ancient vault. I am rushing through your cells, veins, tissues and organs ready to give birth to a new fruit, to myself."

The Snake's hiss transformed into a roar. "The bush! The bush! Go to the blackberry bush. Go through the thick, thorny brush toward the golden purple light where dark, rich, soft and juicy berries are ripe with sensuality, bursting with tartness and awaiting you to swallow their seeds of life."

Snake: "Oh, the thorns. They are protruding and protecting the sweetness and innocence of the berries. It is time for you to melt your armor and take your spirit into the thorny bush. Alena, allow your strong, courageous spirit to lead you to the ripe blackberry bush. Your armor will melt away along your journey. The thorns will stick and prick you. You will bleed. You will bleed freely the deep red blood of your femininity. Give permission for your blood to flow, flowing into Mother Earth to nourish the roots of the sweet berries."

My words fall short expressing the sacredness of my time in therapy and my healing journey. My therapist/teacher/guide and my totem Snake were bridges to my integration and wholeness. I have continued on my path of healing and I am committed to my ongoing growth. I also have been blessed with the many treasures functioning under the archetype of the "wounded healer." I use all of my life experiences of personal healing and restorative skills to facilitate other women's journeys to optimal health, soul and wholeness. I have said *yes* to life.

4.

Depression

Molly, a forty-year-old married woman, was dressed in a casual manner and had magnificent wavy hair that fell just below her shoulders. She wore sandals and a stylish cotton skirt. She used no makeup; her skin was beautiful and had a natural, soft look. Just being in her presence one could sense the gentleness of this earthy, beautiful woman.

Her eyes were moist with tears when she first arrived in my office, but she did not let that discourage her from explaining the situation that prompted her to explore Jungian psychodynamic therapy. She had battled depression for many years, taken a number of different antidepressants and engaged in counseling on more than one occasion with different types of therapy. Since she could not get beyond short-term relief and she was in considerable distress, she elected to pursue the Jungian approach to therapy. She told me her hope was to be able to function without the aid of medication and to find some creative ways to solve the problems she was currently experiencing.

We began by exploring Molly's background and home life. Molly was a mother of two surviving children: a son, fifteen, and a daughter, sixteen. She had previously lost an infant daughter soon after the child's birth. She was also a graduate student at a university studying market research, with the ultimate goal of working in the healthcare field. Her husband was employed as a chemist at a large pharmaceutical firm. Her parents were elderly and in poor health. While her family history suggested the possibility of an inherited trait for depression, she was unhappy in her marriage and felt confined and restricted by the demands of her husband and her parents. The one thing she enjoyed was being a student again. She adored her children and spent much of her time with them.

When her husband arrived home from work, Molly revealed to me, he was often angry and withdrew from the family. No matter how silent and withdrawn he was, he seemed always to be available to his mother, who was his staunchest friend and ally. This behavior was very upsetting to Molly. She had never developed a friendly relationship with her mother-in-law, because she was resentful of the difference between her husband's behavior in the home and his unfailing devotion to his mother. She could not understand why everyone could not coexist as one family. As a result, Molly felt excluded from her husband's relationship with his mother and could not relate to her mother-in-law except on a very superficial level. They avoided each other to the extent that they could.

Whenever her husband withdrew from her and the children, Molly found the situation so stressful that she experienced much physical pain in her back and shoulders, as if to say that the burden on her was too heavy to carry. She had sustained a previous injury to her back, but it appeared that tension seemed to make the pain worse.

I discovered that Molly was very sensitive to criticism and criticism seemed to be what her mother and husband did best. She was the youngest of five children and the only daughter. Her mother did not work outside the home. Her father was employed as a business consultant. Without a doubt, Molly's mother was the dominant parent and her word was law. When a correction or comment was in order, her words were judgmental and blaming. As a result, Molly felt much guilt and shame for having disappointed her mother. Molly learned to expect to be reprimanded or informed in some manner that she or her behavior was less than pleasing to her mother. At the same time, Molly felt her mother to be intrusive and interfering in every aspect of her life even after she became mother to her own children. Growing up, she aligned herself with her father, who was sympathetic and empathetic but powerless to stand up to his wife.

There was a definite difference in Molly's mother's expectations of her sons and her expectations of Molly. The brothers were readily forgiven and excuses were made for their behavior. Rules were much more lenient and even bent for them. In contrast, Molly's mistakes were brought up time and again, as a way of "teaching me to obey the rules." Her mother was a religious person and was very rigid in her belief in the way things *should* be. To defy that philosophy was to earn disapproval and receive a lengthy lecture on the subjects of religion and moral behavior. As a result, Molly's self-esteem suffered and she *expected* people to disapprove of her. "I cannot recall ever feeling good about myself," Molly confided.

When she married, Molly was determined to please her husband in an effort to earn his respect and be accepted as a valued person. She adored her children and instilled in them a love for education. She was the overseer of homework and, in cases when it was needed, she was also their tutor. This meant that regularly scheduled household duties were delayed. Her easygoing way of tending to household chores was a problem for her husband. He functioned best in a home that was tidy at all times, just like his mother's home was always tidy. He expected Molly and the children to conform to his standards.

Molly refused to sacrifice the educational requirements of her children to her husband's need for order and she continued with her program of tutoring after school: papers and books, calculators and laptops scattered about the table notwithstanding. This time, she would not give in to his anger. She also chose to attend to her own assignments to earn her graduate degree. The result was criticism and emotional distancing on her husband's part and conflicted feelings on her part. She was angry. She was frightened. She was weary. She became very anxious and depressed when her husband refused to speak to her for days, because this was the way that her mother had controlled her when Molly dared to defy her. Molly's mother withdrew and did not speak to her when Molly was disobedient, disappointing or otherwise not in good standing. This was horrifying for Molly and, when her husband used the same method of getting her to conform to the rules he set forth, she felt alone and anxious. She felt like a child again!

Another serious problem she told me about was the health of her aging parents. Both her mother and father were suffering with serious, chronic and potentially dangerous illnesses. They were both stubborn and refused treatments prescribed by their physicians, because they felt the treatments were too aggressive and expensive. Neither she nor her brothers could persuade them otherwise. They had always been conservative and were not inclined to change their ways. Since they lived a substantial distance away from Molly, she was worried and concerned for their well-being. Molly took personal responsibility for their care and, as often as she could, she traveled to visit them and attempted to help in any way she could. The journey was long and tedious, but Molly knew that a responsible adult had to be involved in monitoring their care. To help manage the situation, Molly often had her parents visit with her instead.

This was not an easy task, but it did reduce her travel time. As a guest in Molly's home, her mother commented on everything and Molly found herself to be just as tense as when she was a child in her mother's presence. Moreover, her parents made no effort to adjust to the family routine but conducted themselves as guests. Molly found herself trying desperately to entertain them, fulfill her obligations to her family, attend classes at the university and keep up with her assignments. She was exhausted. She began to experience headaches, digestive problems, insomnia and anxiety. The only compassion she received was from her friends, who urged her to seek professional help.

Even though Molly protested the strict environment that her parents valued, she was as conservative with herself as her parents were with her. She found it difficult to indulge herself by giving herself simple, womanly things without being compelled to justify the purchase, no matter how small the amount of money involved or how reasonable it was that she should have them. At the same time, she did not restrict her children or her husband from buying things they might like. It was better not to indulge herself with anything, even trivial things, than to feel the guilt!

The values that rose above the guilt were education for herself and her children. She felt less guilt about educational funding for herself, because she worked part-time to pay some of her tuition costs. Assessing the total picture of Molly's life, she was attempting to fulfill all the obligations of mother, laundress, housekeeper, cook, student, part-time employee, tutor, wife, sister and daughter; and everyone needed everything. The only positive feedback she received was through her friendships outside the home. It was clear to me that Molly was seriously depressed.

Molly related to me that communication with her husband was almost nonexistent except for quarrels and disagreements. She was desperately afraid of his anger and she had little experience of setting boundaries for herself, the children, her parents or her husband. She felt totally suppressed in all areas of her life, with the exception of school. In that intellectual, stimulating environment she excelled and, for the time she was in attendance, she felt like she belonged. By the time she arrived at her home, her mood darkened.

To enter her home, for Molly, was like descending into the darkness. Were it not for her children, she would not have entered at all. But how would she survive without the financial support of her husband? Her present job was subject to school semester schedules. During one of our sessions, Molly shared with me that she had been offered a research position for the next school year. She felt relieved and the world seemed brighter.

To be appointed to the research position was a boost to her self-esteem, but it also meant that she had to meet the requirements and rigors of her graduate program in order to obtain her degree: select a thesis advisor and a committee to oversee her work, write a proposal for her thesis and get the consent of the committee to proceed with her final research project—a large order. The entire process was time consuming. A second requirement was to gain experience in the field of market research by working at least two days a week with supervision for two full semesters, all of which had to be completed before she could present her final research paper for graduation.

The children were not particularly affected by the changing schedules. They were concerned with their own lives. Her daughter had been admitted to the university she had chosen and was preparing to graduate high school. She would be living on campus in a distant state. Her son had a close relationship with both his grandparents and was intent on completing his final two years of high school. He was more concerned with his friends, school and social life. Molly's mother and husband expressed their anger in no uncertain terms. Her mother soundly scolded her and blamed her for not being available when she needed her most. She absolved her sons of any responsibility. Her husband became even more agitated and communication between the spouses was angry and argumentative.

Because of the increasing pressure from her parents and husband, Molly considered giving up the idea of pursuing a higher degree. Up to this point, no matter how much she had to suffer and give of herself, she had steadfastly avoided the suggestion that she set limits for everyone in her life. She had never set limits for anyone but herself. I conveyed to her that it was time for her to do so if she was to reach her own goals.

Molly revealed to me that she had a vision of her future (*her* future, not anyone else's). She realized that she was at her limit and told me she wanted to learn new ways of communicating with her parents and husband. She learned well. Through role-play, we practiced how to keep focused on goals. We practiced how to keep from backsliding under the pressure of an unfair playing field: mother, father and husband on one team and she on the other with no backup. She learned the key words, such as "selfish," that caused her to become defensive. Molly began to realize the gravity of the situation and she learned well how to stand her ground. Her family members were affecting her *future*! She refused to let them do that. It was not her fault that she could not be a carbon copy of her mother-in-law. She was *Molly*, her own person, and she had done a good job with her family. Her children were well equipped to become successful. She learned to admit her faults as well. She could own the fact that she was enabling her parents and her husband to control her by denying her own authentic self in favor of peace, causing her to suffer from major depression.

When major changes are taking place and those changes are frightening, the body begins to react or, one might say, "act up." Molly's back pain increased tremendously. She had to undergo many treatments to be able to function physically. Even though she was suffering excruciating pain, she was determined to go on with her task: declaring her intention to continue her graduate studies and accepting the position the university was offering. It was a time of suffering, a time to allow the pent-up rage to be released. She knew that the pain would stop once she won her independence. Even as she feared the punishment of her parents and husband, she was not to be deterred from the task, pain notwithstanding.

Through our role-play, she learned to speak in the same confident tone of voice she used in other situations, making her statements clear and concise. There would be no backing down! The time had come to set limits and declare her intentions without apology. She was so frightened, but she was also resolved that she would go through with her plan.

Molly first informed her husband and children of her decision. She was somewhat surprised when the children were supportive. Her husband felt and acted differently. He was not encouraging. He listened, then retreated and distanced himself from her.

She had a serious talk with her parents and pointed out to them that it would be in their best interest to seek out medical attention for their problems so that they could take care of many of their needs themselves, because she would not be as available as she had been. Her mother was outraged that she would be so selfish as to abandon them when they needed her the most. She assured them that they would be well cared for by all their children, because her brothers would be helping. Then she spoke individually with each of her brothers about her decision and asked that they take turns and help with the ongoing care of their aging parents. To her surprise, they agreed.

With the resolution of the care situation for her parents, Molly began to feel happy and excited about life. In a few months, her depression was in remission. She was energized and she looked forward to each new day. It was not long before the physical pain was manageable as well.

The problem of her marriage was acute and she began to consider separating from her husband. Her concern was for her son, who was still a high school student. He was well prepared for college and had already been admitted to the school of his choice, but, nonetheless, his well-being as a minor had to be considered. Her children were first and foremost in her mind. She began to waver and slip back into her old pattern of putting herself last. Then she shared with me a dream where her totem and spirit guide revealed itself:

> I know that there is a fourteen-and-one-half-foot snake.
> People are giving the responsibility for its care to me. I
> do not see the snake.

We talked about how Molly had her first encounter with the
Serpent. It is inconsequential that she did not see it. It was there and
she had been charged with caring for it. Psyche had spoken. Her life
was about to change.

As we talked, Molly could not recall a time that she did not feel
guilty. No matter what she wanted, she could not feel good about it.
According to her mother, it was *wrong* to pamper herself. It was *wrong*
to want a life of her own or to spend money on luxury items (no matter that she could afford it or how small the luxury). It was *wrong* to
desire anything if it was for herself. This was the lesson she learned
from her parents and then carried forward into her marriage. Her husband followed suit. He criticized her every attempt to buy anything
that was not his idea. By accepting the research position, Molly would
have her own money. This little bit of freedom to spend her own
money was exhilarating.

Until this time, Molly had suppressed her dreams. With her bold
decision to go forward, it was as if the doors of the unconscious burst
open and the dreams were once again available to her. Molly and I discussed many old dreams and new dreams that came forward into her
consciousness. One she shared revealed her inner male:

> I am in high school. I see a male friend. He recognizes
> me. He is responsive to me. It is as if we are joining
> together. He is gentle, caring and strong. Then I notice
> another male friend from high school. He is accepting
> and tender, too.

Molly was amazed at the sense of peace she experienced after this dream. She had never felt the warmth of being comfortable in her own skin before. Now, the optimal time had arrived to begin the process of change. After Molly made the decision to confront her family and set limits, she performed her tasks with elegance and strength. Such an achievement was monumental for a woman who had been emotional and fearful for as long as she could recall. When she acted with a no-nonsense, firm yet calm attitude, her inner males in the dream were helpful, friendly and accepting. I thought this was a good sign that she was well on her way to achieving her goals through mastery over her emotions in favor of systematically planning her future. Molly's dream world was rich in imagery and she was revisited by a dream she had experienced in the past:

> I am wandering through neighborhoods, peering into
> people's windows. The houses are occupied. A woman
> is sitting on a porch. She gives me a book. It is an
> important book. The inside of the book shows a path,
> a maze. It is a sacred text associated with knowledge,
> ideas and wisdom.

It seemed to me this dream surfaced to remind her of her life's mission. Molly had always felt that she lived on the periphery of life, watching others live the life she would have liked to live were it possible. Therefore, she peered into the lives of others through windows. She was alone. She had walked alone for most of her life. Trust did not come easily for her.

Nonetheless, the woman in her dream appeared to give her the option for life. Who but a wise woman would have access to such a text? Molly felt that the gift was a gift of wisdom. It was hers to use as she saw fit. The book of wisdom would not be ignored. The wise woman would not be ignored. They were gifts for Molly, if she would accept them.

The time had arrived for Molly to make her decision. She had to agree with herself to be the *bad guy*: the part of herself that she could not consciously own or summon to her aid. Being the bad guy meant that she was the one to make the move to separate; she was the one who would be leaving her son behind if he chose not to go with her; she was the one who would not be on call and at the ready to respond to every request her parents made of her and her time. She confided that she was very frightened. She had never before made as decisive a move as this one promised to be. She knew others would use mean and nasty words to define her behavior towards her husband. What would the neighbors think? How would her mother react to the news that she was leaving her family home? What would her father and her children say?

"Sometimes," I suggested to Molly, "we just have to be the bad guy. Sometimes we just have to agree to accept the rain (and the sleet and the hail, if need be); otherwise we may never see a rainbow. When psyche calls, no one is guaranteed an easy journey. To resist the call is to live a half-life. To resist the call is to never fully realize your full potential."

Molly took several deep breaths and then declared that she was up to the task. She began to plan in earnest for a formal separation. Finances were a grave concern but, as so often happens when a commitment to change is made, fate (or whatever one may call it) stepped in and a solution appeared.

In this case, a remarkable offer was presented to her—an offer of a job with a steady salary and with concessions for education. Also, because her research and studies tied in with the advent of managed healthcare, she was sought after to speak before interested groups. This allowed her an opportunity to speak in different locations throughout the country and, best of all, her thesis committee viewed this as valuable experience and considered it to be an asset to her education. She valued the community of friends she had built and her intention was to continue uninterrupted on her own path. This time she would not be alone. The world was Molly's for the taking, fear notwithstanding.

Her children, secure in the knowledge that Molly had been and always would be readily available and supportive of them, made the decision to remain with their father and complete their educations. Surprisingly, her parents were supportive of her although disappointed in the almost certain termination of her marriage. Molly realized that she could do nothing to alleviate her husband's pain. He continued to assign blame to her. She tried to consider the circumstances from his point of view and was able to refrain from breaking down under the weight of the burden she carried. (Being the bad guy is hard!) Her dream told the story of her loneliness as a child, always displaced by her brothers:

> I am in a big building with glass doors. There is a conference going on. Peering out through the glass is Mother, her face wet from crying. I open the door and greet her. Mother is attending a part of the conference on healing. Father is in the background. He is happy about the process of healing. One of my brothers is being healed. My brother will be immortalized in the book called *Daddy's Book*.

Molly's impression of the landscape of this dream was that it reminded her of her own family as a cultish-type family system. She felt safe only because she was free to move in and out of the building. That she was intent on being free suggested that she felt more like a prisoner than a willing participant in the family system. She was not directly involved in the ceremony of healing that celebrated her brother. It appeared that she was outside the circle of the family. Her mother and father were on the other side of the glass window. The ceremony was already taking place or would be taking place shortly.

Her mother was profoundly moved and her father was in the background (as he had always been in Molly's life), kind and loving parent that he was. Father was happy on this momentous day. His son was being immortalized! What was clear was that Molly stood apart from the celebration and when she entered the big building with glass doors, she mentally prepared herself to escape or, at best, avoid the family if she could not leave. She was not able to connect in a meaningful way with her father.

Molly's experience of the family had always been uncomfortable. In the dream, as in real life, when entering into the confines of the family system, she kept one eye on the door at all times, needing to be sure that she could escape if she had to. Spontaneity was not one of Molly's strong traits. One cannot be spontaneous and vigilant at the same time. She had to *know* the way out.

Molly felt that her parents had always deferred to her brothers. The brother from her dream was a younger brother and seemed always to be in good standing with their parents. He had never been, nor was he at the time of this dream, subject to the same restrictions and penalties that kept Molly ever conscious of how her behavior would be interpreted or accepted by her mother. On the contrary, her brother's behavior often gave her parents cause for concern, but they tolerated and excused his indiscretions.

On this day, however, her brother was to be healed and immortalized in *Daddy's Book*. Molly expressed to me that the healing ceremony and her brother's reward felt like a repetition of the ordinary course of events. As with the biblical prodigal son, her brother was celebrated when he did things right and forgiven when he flaunted all the rules. It was evident that she was resentful and emotionally distant from the whole event. Molly was there, as she was required to be. She showed little empathy for her mother's tears and only observed her father in the background. She made no spontaneous moves toward either of them. Instead, she kept in mind that she was free to move in and out of the rooms.

I wondered, *Why this dream now?* She had been given the gift of the book of wisdom from the wise woman. She was in the process of making the necessary arrangements to move on with her life. She had accepted a position that did not interfere with her educational goals. Both her parents had accepted her decision. Life was moving along, but what of the old feelings and resentments that lay in the unconscious that had not been resolved? They were moving right along with her, as well. Psyche, in its infinite wisdom, brought to consciousness unfinished business, allowing Molly the opportunity to recognize and address the problems of her childhood that influenced the way she lived in the world as an adult. Molly's resolve to move on was strong, although she was weary. Despite all this and her determination, Molly still had setbacks. While her parents conceded that they were supportive of her decisions, they offered her no other support. In fact, they worried, often out loud for Molly to hear, about what would happen to them now. Her husband was angry and blamed her for the failure of their marriage. Her children were focused on their own goals and although part of her knew this was a good thing, the other part felt abandoned by them as well. Why didn't they care?

The dream focused on the preferential treatment that her brother had always received and she could not help but compare herself with him at this juncture in her life. She felt that if this were her brother's situation, her parents would be offering financial aid or any other kind of support he might need. She could, of course, ask them for financial support, but she refused to do so, taking into account their health status and the increased costs of aging. That she was also dealing with her own abandonment issues was evident in this dream. She was as alone as she had ever been and she was resentful because of the lack of *real* support from her parents. "Aren't parents supposed to be there?" she questioned.

This dream gave Molly the opportunity to address all the old angers and resentments that lay in her unconscious. "When we navigate the path toward growth and independence," I observed to Molly in one of our sessions, "we travel alone. Sometimes, this can be hard to accept when there are parents whom you feel are *supposed* to love you and be there for you and weep for you, too, not only for your brother."

At this juncture, I asked Molly what she needed. She broke down in tears and replied: "I need love." Love from the outside is tenuous at best. What Molly had never learned was how to love *herself*. She deprived herself of everything that she could possibly do without in the interest of being frugal. Hadn't her mother told her many times that humility was virtuous? Molly gave freely of her love to her children and, initially, to her husband. She gave freely of herself to her parents as best she could. She supported her brothers when support was indicated. She had not asked for help from her family until this time and she felt that her parents were giving her the minimal amount of support. She was comparing herself unfavorably with her younger brother and the level of support that would be available to him in the same situation.

I asked Molly what she needed from her parents. She responded: "Love." How, then, did Molly define *love*? Her father worked and provided a home for his family. Was this love? He was readily available to her and sometimes even joined forces with her in negotiating a deal with her mother. Was this love? He was kind and considerate. Was this love? He avoided confrontation with his wife rather than defend her. Was this love? Would it have been better to witness disagreement between her parents?

Molly's mother maintained a lovely home for the family. Was this love? She expected and demanded excellence of Molly and, to some extent, her brothers. Was this love? Her mother was focused on her own needs for her children and herself, to the exclusion of their individual preferences. Was this love? Her mother could be cold, demanding and withholding of her affections if she did not get what she wanted. Was this love? Her mother was happy when Molly was catering to her in some way. Was this love?

Is the definition of love each person's own perception of what love should be?

When I probed deeper into the mother/daughter and father/daughter relationships Molly had with her parents, she was able to see that her parents were human beings with their own problems. Their lives did not begin with their marriage and the birth of their children. They brought to the table of marriage all that had existed before in their own family relationships. They brought their expectations, fears and beliefs with them and these would, in turn, be visited on their children, including Molly.

Molly learned and eventually accepted that her mother's belief in the absolute authority of the parent was a product of her own experience of growing up in a family where absolute authority was the rule. Moreover, this position was supported by Molly's father, who bowed to her mother's authority in the interest of peace. Molly's mother's value for excellence (according to her own interpretation of excellence), little tolerance for dissent and narrow view of the world were the products of the experience of her own family while growing up. Her mother felt privileged and expected extraordinary treatment as a sign of respect for authority; I suspected a possible self-absorbed personality. With regard to the belief in more leniency for the boys, the saying "boys will be boys" came to mind.

None of this has anything to do with Molly as a person. She was merely born into the family as it was. This is true of all of us. The task of maturing is to strive to become your own person even if it goes against the culture and belief system of your family. Molly's task was not yet completed. She was defined by the way she was being treated by others. If anyone expressed displeasure with her, she was crushed. If anyone expressed pleasure with her, she was affirmed. She continued to believe that if she did not cater to the demands of her parents then she was inferior as a daughter. It was not surprising that she had suffered with depression for years.

When we first encounter a dream such as Molly's *Daddy's Book* dream, we may wonder *why now?* Now may be the best time, in fact! It is better to go on the newfound path toward being all we can be without the burden of the old troublesome fears and resentments. It is to our advantage at any time in our lives to face our demons and dissect them one by one, to throw them to the winds and walk freely along the path that takes us to new beginnings. To do so is to provide the climate for growth and realize our own authentic selves, regardless of individual opinions.

"The unconscious brings to consciousness the task of con-fronting painful old beliefs," I told Molly as we discussed her dream. This dream *Daddy's Book* was unfinished business for Molly. It brought to her the need to understand the experiences of her parents and how these experiences impacted her life. It brought to her the need to give due respect to the task set upon her parents to provide for the children they had birthed. It brought to her the sacrifices her parents made to meet the goals set out for them and to raise responsible adults in the best way they knew. (We learn parenting by our own experiences of being children.) It brought to her the need to accept her parents for who they were and, if possible, to forgive them their trespasses.

Daddy's Book was a very moving experience for Molly. She wept as we worked through the dream. She had never before thought of her parents as children themselves, subject to parental influences. She was grateful that, in her own home, there existed no authoritarian ruler. Both she and her husband were available for their children and they, in turn, were encouraged with parental support to excel to the best of their abilities. The messages the children received were upbeat and affirming and they were thriving in this climate.

In the course of her therapy with me, Molly learned that her thoughts, attitudes and behaviors *influenced* others, including family. If she expected to be treated badly, her attitude and body language gave the family (or anyone else, for that matter) the cues and she would be subject to disapproving attitudes and behaviors as well. On the other hand, if she was expecting to have fun and relax with her family, her attitude and body language generated this kind of feeling in others. What we give, we get back in return.

Molly learned that when she was to be in the presence of her parents, either in her home or theirs, *she was to be conscious of her own feelings about the possibilities that might occur there*. Was she feeling badly because of her past experience? Or was this a *new* experience that she could influence simply by monitoring her own thoughts, expectations and behaviors *before* she encountered her parents or family? As we worked together, Molly learned to *monitor* her own feelings and attitude and take *responsibility* for herself.

Molly was now better equipped to acknowledge the blessings she already had both as a student and as an employee: good friends, a job, the ability to take her leave from a very painful marriage, good health, a supportive dissertation committee and recognition of her work. She was in a very good place.

The next task she faced was to leave her home and the community she had come to love and relocate to a home of her own. Fear and sadness were very much a part of this process, but she knew she had to go. The *knowing* was well beyond the intellectual recognition that she was on another path. The knowing came with the book of wisdom. There was an element of destiny that produced a sense of the inevitable path she must take, regardless of the sacrifices that this journey required along the way.

"When the Serpent appears," I reminded Molly, "she also provides the means to negotiate the course. The wise woman walks with you and provides you with the lessons contained in the book of wisdom to make way for the woman you are destined to be. You accepted the book and, in doing so, you accepted the challenge." We discussed how grief was a natural part of the process of change. Just as in nature, there would be no spring without the winter, and so it was with Molly. She was experiencing her own dark night of the soul.

While Molly recognized that life had changed drastically, she was beset with fear for her future and grief for the losses she was experiencing. She considered giving up on her dissertation. She could not think with clarity about school when her life was falling apart at the seams, even though she knew that she could not go back and pick up the pieces. She could not believe that her marriage had come to this. She was immersed in the grief process and she would not emerge until she had reached resolution.

For a number of years, Molly had denied the sad state of her marriage and family life. Even as she made the decision to end her marriage, she could not accept that the end was near. Maybe she could try harder. Maybe she could talk with her husband and come to some sort of consensus on how to communicate better. Each of her attempts to determine how she could recover the marriage was met with a dead end.

It was only later that she owned the anger that she felt. Molly was angry with everyone: her parents, her husband, his family, her family, her academic requirements. She held her feelings tightly. She did not give any visible indication of the pressure she was feeling. However, inwardly she was miserable. Finally, she got angry enough to justify going ahead with her plan to relocate. Change is hard, but fortunately, at this opportune time, a dream helped to clarify the situation for her:

> I am in a place with my husband's parents. There is a little narrow path. It is a garden path. It is his mother's garden. It is very hard to walk along this little path. My husband's father is complaining and accusing me of giving him a heart attack.

Molly felt that she had always walked a narrow path to meet the expectations of her mother and those of her husband and his family. To deviate from the path was not an option for her; any infractions that earned displeasure from the authority figures in her life caused her to feel tremendous fear, guilt and blame. If she went through with her life plan, then she was guilty for causing distress or worse (heart attacks can kill) in the family. Internalized guilt and blame such as this were compelling.

How could she go on with her plan and be the bad guy with so much hanging over her head? Was it true that she had the power to arrest a person's heartbeat? Or was it true that she was losing sight of her plan, giving in to her fear and insecurity instead of planning her life? If so, the man in her dream was going to be cranky and mean-spirited. She had slipped back into emotional turmoil and the dream told her so directly, I analyzed. That is the way of growth; we go forward two steps and go back one.

The path Molly was on was very difficult to negotiate. She could hardly stay on it. The dream was telling her something. It was showing her that she could not negotiate this narrow path any longer. It was time for her to confront her own resistance to change, to challenge the notion that if she took care of and loved herself that something very bad would happen to someone and it would be her fault. She just didn't know. She was exhausted. She could not attend to the requirements of her dissertation committee and furthermore, she entertained the thought that she could not, after all, go forward with her studies. Her dream helped to make her journey clearer and easier:

> My daughter and I are trying to get somewhere. There is a huge hole filled with water. It is deep and spreads out wider and wider. There are pilings across the water. People are afraid to walk across. My daughter and I start to walk across. There is a rope to hold on to. It is easy once we get started.

In the dream, Molly saw herself taking the risk and crossing over the hole filled with water. This hole was deep and was spreading out, perhaps implying the longer she waited the harder it would get. In the dream, once she began, she found the task to be easy. In our discussion of the dream, we noted that she left the other people behind.

The dream rope appeared to be the anchor Molly needed to go forward to her own destiny. That her daughter accompanied her suggested that Molly was not abandoning her. Together they walked across. The journey was an adventure that involved them both.

The nature of the water Molly had to cross was not of the life-giving kind. This water was menacing, deep, dark and growing ever wider as she considered what her options were: to remain where she was or go forward? This water was the water of death and for her to be swallowed up in it would be equivalent to her position in the family: swallowed up. That psyche provided a rope was significant. It was time! She had to make the decision to cross over and the rope would be steady and strong for her. Once decided, she found the task to be easy. Symbolically, she was keeping close to her daughter, no matter the distance between them. She was not abandoning her. The child was a willing partner in the journey. This was a good thing. Molly worried for her children even though they were comfortable with the new living arrangements. The dream seemed to tell her "not to worry. She is with you and you are with her. You travel this road together."

Molly's reaction to the dream was to recognize that the time for the journey had arrived and very soon after the dream she made her final arrangements to leave for her new job and new home. She had finally come to resolution and she wanted to act quickly in the interest of settling in before the next school term. Her next dream predicted and lit the way for her:

I am working in a church. I am to mark the envelopes
until the task is completed. I notice a fat candle. It is
brown and grey speckled. A voice says: "You have

enough degrees already. You should get recognition.
Wash it if it gets dirty."

Molly was given the gift of light to show her the way. I explained,
"Symbolically, light is of the sun, the gift of enlightenment." The
dream charged her with maintaining the light, meaning maintaining
her resolve and the vision of her future with clarity (wash the candle
if it gets dirty). If the candle got dirty, then it was possible that the
light would dim and her way would not be as clear. She had to attend
to the light and be conscious of her journey. To give in to the
overwhelming feelings of guilt, shame and blame would dim the light
and the journey would be more difficult. The dream also predicted
recognition. Molly's feelings about the dream and its inherent meaning
were a cross between humility and excitement. She was afraid to get
"too happy." Nonetheless, she could not really hide her joy.

Molly relocated. She prepared a lovely, modest home for herself
and had frequent visitors, including her children. She visited them
often at their respective schools, as did their father. She earned her
graduate degree and gained the recognition that she so earnestly
sought. Her knowledge and expertise as an advocate for healthcare in
the interest of the consumer were then and continue to be in demand.
She forged meaningful relationships and remained friendly with the
father of her children. He adjusted well to the reorganization of the
family, secure in the knowledge that he had earned the love and respect
of his children.

Her parents adjusted even better than expected and Molly
remained mindful of their maintenance and care, responding to their
needs without anger or resentment. She even learned to enjoy making
her parents' days happier when she could. She was able to give and
receive love in a way she had never before experienced and she was
having fun!

When I asked Molly if she wanted to write a few words to describe what therapy meant to her, she declined on the basis that she did not want to look back. She was focused on going forward on her life path. Once she was established in her new home, she wrote me a long and detailed letter about the experience of relocating and settling into her new home. In the letter she wrote what I believe sums up her experience: "I'm in the light now and I like it."

5.

Harassment

When Katie, a forty-five-year-old woman, walked into my office, I could imagine her being on a runway, modeling a beautiful line of women's business clothing. Her suit and hair were impeccable. Shoes, handbag and accessories were just right for an executive's day at the office. When she smiled, her eyes sparkled and her face took on a radiance that one rarely sees in a first encounter with someone. There was no indication of anxiety. She appeared to know exactly what she wanted and needed and she did not hesitate to describe the problem that prompted her to seek a therapist.

Two years ago to the day, her father passed away after a lingering illness. Six months later her mother suddenly passed away from an aneurism. Katie was having a difficult time accepting the deaths of her parents, especially the unexpected death of her mother. Her pain was more acute, because the family home would soon be sold. The loss of the family home seemed to renew the terrible feeling of sorrow that she felt just after her parents died. Her sadness was beginning to impact her ability to concentrate on her work. She felt that she was not coming to terms with her grief and was failing to reach resolution of her losses. Katie was very concerned with the possible loss of business opportunities and the economic consequences if she did not come to resolution.

I asked Katie to begin by telling me about her family dynamics as a child. She was one of two children. Her brother was five years younger than she. Because of the difference in age, they did not have common interests growing up but did have a close brother-sister relationship as adults. Her mother and father were married at an early age and both were business owners. Her father owned a contracting business and her mother owned a modest neighborhood shop in the small town where she was born. While her father tolerated his wife's business interests, he tended to attempt to interfere with the management of her shop. Katie's mother jealously guarded her turf and many arguments ensued between the two. Katie was very protective of her mother and often battled her father to protect her mother's right to run her business as she saw fit. Katie was the buffer between her father's domineering ways and her mother's defensiveness. There was no physical abuse involved, although her parents conducted heated arguments on a regular basis.

Despite her disagreements with her father, from the age of thirteen Katie was an unofficial partner in his business. She learned to manage the business with him, surpassed him in ability and eventually took a leadership role. She was able to manage it on her own by the time she was eighteen years of age.

Katie's father was not inclined to compliment his family. Although he was a very versatile and talented man and an excellent provider, he was more likely to criticize or act out verbally within the family confines. His anger was poorly disguised.

It seemed to Katie that she could do nothing right. She felt that it was impossible to please him. No matter how well she performed as a student or as a woman who owned and operated her own business, her efforts went unrecognized. He was all too ready to criticize her, both professionally and personally, for any reason he could find. Katie could not recall ever hearing her father say that he loved her until a few days before his death. On that momentous day, right before he died, he confessed his love for her and apologized for his behavior toward her through the years. There was neither time nor opportunity for her to realize before he died that he truly loved her.

Katie's relationship with her mother was complicated, she told me. Her mother was cautious and conservative about almost everything. She did not venture far from her home and refused to travel in a plane. She was meek in the presence of her husband in the home. In operating her business, she was dynamic and outgoing. Katie felt that her mother had two personalities: one who was the traditional wife and mother and the other who was a successful, shrewd business owner. The key seemed to be whether or not Katie's father was present or involved. If he was present, she bowed to his demands. This behavior infuriated Katie. She liked the dynamic mother best.

As she witnessed her father's bullying tactics, Katie's heroic self proceeded to defend her mother against his criticism. Katie longed for her mother to engage with her in a mother-daughter activity, such as a fun weekend together, but her mother refused. The only exception was that once, in an effort to escape her husband's anger, Katie's mother stayed overnight with her. To Katie, her mother's meekness was frustrating and, at the same time, she felt sad that her mother was cheated out of the joy of living by the demands of her father.

Katie's frustration with her mother was understandable. In the home, her mother was the opposite of Katie: passive, long-suffering and compliant. Katie, on the other hand, had always been outgoing, dynamic, verbal and fearless. Katie made no secret of how she despised her mother's position as the underdog with her father. Outside the home her mother was also a cause for puzzlement. There, she was on par with Katie and held her own, steadfastly refusing help from anyone.

To me it seemed that Katie approved of her mother's resolve in business, but she strongly identified with her father and she did not apologize for her no-nonsense way of being in the world. She also identified with Athena, the ancient Greek goddess of wisdom, strategy and mediation.[1] Katie certainly used good judgment in planning and developing a successful business; however, the problem was that too much emphasis was on the business end of things and little was left for her soft, feminine self to be realized. She gave others the impression that she was very logical and fixed in her opinions, with little room for empathy or compassion. This attitude often resulted in quarrelsome relationships in her life.

Katie left home to attend college and, upon the completion of her bachelor's degree in economics, she developed a consulting business of her own. Later, she acquired a second business as a financial planner. When she could, she also assisted her father. Her mother continued to refuse any offer of help. She preferred to manage on her own. Katie did not take this situation personally. She understood the importance of her mother's independence and respected her wishes.

A few years after graduating from college Katie married. There were many problems in the relationship. She decided to divorce after two years of misery.

Eventually, she married a second time, only to learn that her second husband was suffering with an addiction. He refused treatment and proceeded to spend any funds available to him to find comfort and escape in the drug. He made no effort to conceal his addiction as their life together unfolded. He became angry when Katie tried to encourage him to get professional help and she came to fear his anger. Katie found this behavior intolerable and, within three years, elected to divorce once again. She picked up the pieces of her life and moved on, even more intent on being successful in the business world. On the outside, Katie was the model of self-sufficiency, direct and sure of herself, but her dream reveals what was on the inside:

I am on the front porch of a large, older house. I am
playing the piano. I look to the right and see a man is
walking toward me. I keep playing. I turn around quickly
and the man is ready to grab me.

Katie's childhood home was a large, old house with a porch. The
dream revisited the place of her youth. I commented to Katie, "I wonder what is left for you to work through from your experience there."
She lived in a rural area and front porches were safe. Not so with this
front porch. She was hyper-alert, watchful and apprehensive. The
"man" was a predator and he was at the ready to grab her from
behind. The dream was a replay of her relationship with her father.
Her childhood home was unsafe. She could not predict her father's
anger, criticisms or demands so she had to keep her wits about her,
for he could "come from behind" and "grab her" with his criticisms
and complaints. Her mother could do nothing to save her; therefore,
Katie had to have a sixth sense and be alert to danger, even on the tran-
quil front porch of her familiar home.

Katie recognized that she was vulnerable and had unresolved
issues with both parents. She also recognized that she was just as
driven as her father and sometimes too abrupt. She agreed that she
needed to make some significant changes and be more available to
others without the benefit of the armor of her heroine, Athena.

Katie was an engaging, social woman. It was not unusual for her
to have male friends in several different areas of the country. She had
no problem keeping track of each of the men with whom she had
developed close relationships, giving each his place in the sun. She was
not promiscuous by any stretch of the imagination; she merely had
the power to enchant men. She had no interest in exploiting these relationships nor did she allow herself to be exploited.

Katie told me of a deep friendship she developed with a man
with whom she had personal and business connections. Initially they

met in college and had known each other for some time before they
went their separate ways. As they got reacquainted after meeting again
after so many years, their relationship developed into a cordial, warm
friendship.

Contrary to her experience of being married and twice divorced,
her friend David had never married and, furthermore, expressed no
interest in changing his lifestyle. Nonetheless, Katie was very attracted
to him, but she respected his position and she contented herself with
his friendship. He was the one she could call when she made an important business decision or if she just needed confirmation or encouragement. One could say that David was the first man in Katie's life
who respected her intelligence and wisdom and who accepted,
affirmed and supported her without reservation or judgment. This
experience was so different from what she had known with her father
and her husbands. She realized that he was the only man she could
trust implicitly.

At the time Katie decided to seek my help, she had been
appointed to chair a charitable organization temporarily until a permanent chairperson could be found. She was well known as a speaker
and organizer and she would be the *acting* chair. The organization provided fully paid job training programs to children who were unable
to master the requirements for college-level work and who were in
the lower income range. This invitation was very moving for Katie
since she had no children of her own. She happily accepted the position and looked forward to making a difference in the lives of children.
She just *knew* she could make such a difference.

What she did not know was that all the board members were men
and, before her appointment, no woman had ever served as the chairperson. When Katie met with the board the first time, she was uncon-
cerned about the composition of the board and did not even consider
this to be a potential problem. After all, she had worked with her father
in business since she was in her teens. Besides, she believed the men
who served on the board were professionals. Together, they held the

interests of the children above all else. Taking on such a huge responsibility was different for Katie. She had never chaired such a large
organization before. It was at this time that she met her totem:

> I am back in senior high school. But it seems to be
> unfamiliar. There are snakes in the hall and in various
> rooms. One is a spice color. It is beautiful and just
> hanging out. My girlfriend kicks the snake. She then
> continues to walk down the hall. There are more snakes
> in the auditorium.

Not only did Katie meet her totem, but she also met her own
brute-like nature in the dream: the nasty girl who was mean to the
beautiful Serpent. She was cold and unfeeling, injuring a creature of
nature without remorse or guilt. This was contrary to Katie's experience of herself. Even though she considered herself to be an Athena
warrior woman—competitive and ready for a fight if attacked—she
had never been known to pick fights or lash out without reason. Just
the thought of being so angry and uncaring proved to be unsettling
to her.

"There are two sides to everything," I told Katie. "When we
meet a same-sex person in a dream, we are symbolically meeting a
part of ourselves that we do not yet know." Katie did not know herself
as nasty and mean. Her method of solving problems was to make use
of strategy, plotting and planning her moves. No matter; Serpent, as
totem, announces that the time has come for change. Change and
healing are the gifts of the Serpent spirit guide when the challenge is
met. With the appearance of the Serpent, one can expect to encounter
tasks that require courage and, oftentimes, loss or death to the old
before the new can live and be realized. Change requires stamina, sacrifice and hard work. Katie would soon realize how compelling the
pressures would be in this new adventure she had agreed to take on.
But why did the mean girl and the Serpent appear in her dreams at
this particular time?

It was just at this point that Katie was preparing to enter the world of men as the leader of the group. This was significantly different from the one-on-one interactions with her father in his business environment. Besides, there was yet another dimension of her relationship to her father: She was the *star*, Daddy's girl. That she would be the first female chairperson was a challenging situation, but she was fearless and comfortable with her decision to accept the challenge.

Katie was not one to shirk her responsibility, so she took it upon herself to learn more about the organization and then, as the search for a permanent chairperson was being conducted, she proceeded to prove that she was the best nominee for that position.

Initially, the members of the board were cordial. Although Katie announced her interest in a permanent appointment, the board members did not react in any way that was noticeable. However, when Katie was actually nominated for the permanent position, the polite, social atmosphere of the board meetings changed.

The meetings were conducted in the same room with the same people, but the mood shifted. When Katie attempted to open a discussion on a topic to be considered, the members challenged her, interrupted her and generally became so unruly that nothing could really be accomplished. Katie was confused by this radical change in behavior, but she attempted to "ride it out" until she could determine what was happening.

The behavior of the board members became unmanageable and embarrassing. Outside speakers were often invited to the meetings to present ideas, discuss the current state of affairs of charitable organizations or provide inventive ways of fundraising in the interest of the children who would benefit from such fundraising efforts. On one occasion, Katie had asked a female lecturer to speak on ways to generate income to provide the organization with what it needed to meet its goals. To her embarrassment, certain board members were disrespectful and challenged each and every statement the guest speaker put forth for discussion, making it impossible for her to present her ideas. There were members who did not take part in the harassment, but neither did they interfere or protest the many interruptions to the discussion.

Katie's response to this behavior was anger. This warrior woman drew her sword and stood ready to do battle with her tormenters. She lectured them soundly on matters of etiquette and then urged her guest to continue to speak. The board members, obviously taken aback by the scolding, listened politely but would not participate in post-lecture questions and discussions. This behavior infuriated Katie even more and future meetings were described by Katie as "tugs of war." Who was winning the war? Katie shared a new dream that revealed the struggle:

> My father, mother and I are in a car. Father is driving
> from the backseat. I get out of my seat to drive. My
> father jumps out of the car and threatens to leave me.
> He doesn't leave me.

Katie's battle with the members of the board was very much like two armies battling with each other. She was not winning the war, just as she did not win the "war" with her father. I analyzed that the dream symbolically showed her where she was: in a very vulnerable position. If she did not comply with the board members' wishes, she could be ousted from her venerable position of chairperson. Katie would be best served by using less confrontational tactics to fight her battle with the board. "There is more than one way to fight a war," I observed and Katie agreed. It is always best to take a dream message seriously and Katie took hers very seriously. She was ready to learn a more refined way of managing the board members.

With practice and role-play, Katie learned to *stop and think* before she responded to the remarks made by the members of the board. She learned to *repeat the statement* made before she attempted to respond. Katie also understood that she *did not have to respond immediately*; she could simply table the issue until a later date, delaying her reply. In addition we practiced how to *respond in a positive manner*. Whenever

Katie presented a proposal for discussion, the board's reaction was to try to sabotage the idea, for example: "That will never work," "It's been tried before" or "Good luck with that one." Sarcasm was plentiful. Katie planned to *acknowledge the observations*, then introduce the idea that the proposal could be of interest to try anyway and see what happened. She vowed to *smile more often* and greet her fellow board members warmly instead of with a frozen half-smile.

After Katie implemented these changes, the harassment took on a different dimension. Sexual comments were made, causing her considerable worry. How should she respond to sexual comments in such an environment? She was troubled and concerned. Her dream seemed to compensate for the bitter harassment she was experiencing:

> I am lying on the ground. I had been at a meeting in
> Boston. Then I get up and put the car in the garage.
> A cowboy is concerned for me and the contents of my
> purse. He picks me up and carries me home to take care
> of me. I am wearing a gorgeous creamy white
> shimmering gown, but he is not wearing a tux. He lays
> down a caftan and carries me across the threshold. Then
> I am in a house at a party and people are conversing
> with me.

We discussed whether this was the same warrior woman who carried a sword and did not hesitate to use it if provoked. Yes, I analyzed, it was yet another part of the personality that had revealed itself in the dream: the soft, vulnerable princess. It would be nice to be rescued from the harassment she was experiencing. Yet, even as her cowboy prince was at her service, she was critical of him. He did not meet her *full* criteria for a prince. Just as her father could never find her good enough, she did not find the prince good enough. Katie was the apple of her father's eye, the beautiful princess even as she did battle with him. He indulged her nonetheless. Katie knew her place with her father and it was a far better place than her mother held. On the other hand, both she and her mother were subject to his criticism—nothing was ever good enough. When we are exposed to the same situation over and over again, even if we do not like the situation, we may unconsciously do the same things without realizing it. So it was with Katie and the dream let her know about it.

Katie's father was never really satisfied. Similarly, the dream princess was petulant and critical toward the prince. Nonetheless, the fairy tale had a happy ending: The heroine was attending a party and others were relating well to her. She was not in a power struggle here. The party represented her relationship to people and to life. She was in a pleasant social gathering, a place where she excelled and was most comfortable.

Katie's response to this rejected side of her personality was one of disbelief. She could not imagine herself being "carried" anywhere. The dream cannot lie. It bares our souls, our truths, our hopes and our dreams without concern for our feelings or beliefs. While Katie could not imagine herself as narcissistic and self-absorbed, she did admit that as the only daughter she was indulged and that she took this favored position for granted. The dream exposed the soft, vulnerable part of her as well and Katie would do well to own this part of her personality, no matter that she detested what she perceived to be a weakness. Warrior women value strength above all else. It was understandable that she was distressed and humiliated by the behaviors of the board members and longed for rescue.

Despite all that was going on, her popularity increased with a few supporters in the community. The excitement of her nomination was heady. Katie was gaining more control of the meetings and felt confident that she would be the choice for permanent chairperson. The board members did not share her enthusiasm and the vicious attacks against her became more frequent. In her next dream, Katie shared more of this struggle:

I am in an upstairs room. My friend is with me. He is a
guest. I go upstairs to the bathroom. The door is closed.
I cannot open it. It is stuck. I push it open. A male hand
holding a gun pushes its way through the opening and
he shoots me. My friend hears the shot and screams
my name.

In this dream, Katie was in her family home where she was both
glorified (Daddy's girl) and scorned (can't do anything right). Everything was an effort. The door was stuck and who knew what lurked
behind it? In this case, danger and possible death were hidden behind
the door. Katie and I could not rule out the effect the attitudes of the
male members of the board were having on her psyche. Katie was
being attacked from all angles, yet her investment in becoming chairperson did not falter, even if it killed her in the end as in her dream.
The effect of the dream lingered long after the actual dream occurred.
She told me she was frightened and concerned with such a horrible
dream. She had reason to be concerned: the dream predicted violence
against her.

One night, soon after this violent dream, Katie awakened to the
sound of the phone ringing. The caller identified himself as a member
of the board and threatened her if she continued in her pursuit of
chairing the organization. He would not accept a woman heading this
traditionally male-dominated organization. Katie was shaken, realizing
that the dream she had recently experienced was a predictive dream.
Someone out there was already thinking of harming her to preserve
male leadership of the organization.

At our next meeting, I could see Katie was having a difficult time
concealing her confusion and distress given these latest developments.
She seemed to be crumbling. As if by some mighty internal force, she
remained resolute. On the other hand, she threatened to "let loose"
with all the anger she was suppressing in the interest of being logical
and professional. Her cool, strategic, intellectual Athena-self was

hanging on the edge! She needed much support to go on with the task of being elected chairperson, since this was her choice despite all of the obstacles in her way.

An older member of the board apparently had seen and heard enough to step up and publicly compliment her efforts on behalf of the goals set by the organization. Since he was a highly respected member of the community, the other board members became more cautious and, from that point, refrained from harassing Katie in the meetings. Her dream expressed her relief that *someone* on the board was kind and protective:

> I am in bed with my rescuer, the man who spoke up at the meeting. He is holding me in a protective way.

In this dream, Katie's armor was coming off. She was vulnerable and hurt, content to be held. Katie was sad and bewildered by the dynamics occurring in her life, but she would not give up the dream she held of making a difference in the lives of the children in her charge. Her attitude became more resolute and less militant at this point. I noticed that her manner of speaking had softened, but she expressed that she was afraid of the vulnerability that she was experiencing. Even though Katie was uncomfortable with the events that were occurring in her life, the opportunity for growth was presenting itself in the meltdown of the armor on which she depended to protect her from the negative forces in her life. In the end, Katie was named to chair the organization.

Katie was very serious and intent on preserving the integrity and financial stability of the program and just as intent on keeping the power she had worked so diligently to acquire. An internal battle raged on. She loathed that she was more vulnerable than she had ever been and she felt trapped in the endless cycle of competition. This was unknown territory for her. She dreamed a series of dreams she shared with me that revealed her totem's attempts to guide her:

I am at a social event. Snakes are all over the carpet.
I am not afraid.

I said to Katie, "We know that when the Serpent appears in the
dream, a task is at hand whether the dreamer is ready or not." Katie
stated she was up to the task, but she was on the edge of regressing
to her more primitive, angry, undisciplined self. The serpents seemed
to be docile and ready to "be there" for her.

She felt unsettled and anxious but still would not back down.
Her dream's spirit guides seemed to be very vigilant and protective of
her:

I am on a wharf. Snakes are all around me. I am not afraid.

This dream took place near the water. The serpents surrounded
her, encasing her in a circle and protecting her from harm. The circle
was a *mandala*, the ageless symbol of "psychic wholeness."[2] She felt
no fear of her totem serpents. She was calm in their presence. Water,
such as the deep waters of the ocean, suggested that this dream went
deeper than the ordinary daily events in her life. The powerful symbols
of the circle, the Serpent and the deep waters implied a protection
around her that went beyond the ordinary. One might say that this
was the sacred protection of the Divine. Katie felt relieved after this
dream and ventured forward, confident and unafraid.

Now, with the influential board member's support, Katie was
able to conduct meetings in a reasonable manner. But things were not
as they seemed. Katie noticed a subtle change taking place in the board
meetings and she realized that her friend on the board had his own
agenda. Craftily, he began to plan how topics of interest would be for-
mulated and introduced to the members. His suggestions were often
self-serving. At first Katie felt that they were not really in competition
with her own goals for the organization, but nonetheless, they were

his ideas superimposed on hers. Moreover, he kept suggesting that he would always be there for her beyond the support she needed from him within the board.

Katie's level of discomfort was increasing. Her primary task as chairperson was to plan an event to increase revenue. As hard as it was for her, she contented herself with learning ways to avoid his advances and (in her words) "buy time" before introducing suggestions that she felt were in the interest of her own goals. Katie's intent was to secure enough money in donations to keep the program afloat and, in so doing, preserve the educational program for the children. Her totem Serpent did not abandon her. It made its presence known in her new dream:

> I see a snake. It is regal. It has smooth white skin that sparkles. It is adorned with colorful jewels. I am in its presence and humbled by its beauty and power.

Katie had encountered the divine Serpent: the Serpent of healing, wisdom and transformation. She was in a sacred place where all things had the potential for coming together and she was awed and reverent in the Serpent's presence. Katie's dreams were occurring in rapid succession and she shared another with me:

> I am on location making a movie. I go into a church. I walk from the lobby into the aisle. I notice rare coins. I hold them. I know that I have to keep them safe. My role calls for me to disappear. A priest is there in full ceremonial dress for the Mass that is about to take place.

In our therapy sessions I explored with Katie how she was once again given the sacred symbols to protect her, even though she was supposed to disappear. She was in a sacred place: a church. In this church were the coins that were to be in her keeping. Coins, because of their circular shape, are symbols of the mandala. To keep them safe was to keep herself safe, despite the poorly disguised efforts to make her disappear. The celebrant priest was to perform the sacred rite of the Mass, a symbol of transformation and renewal.

After these dreams, Katie was so energized that she felt like she had been given a new life. She methodically and brilliantly went about planning a charitable event that was incredibly ambitious for a newly elected chairperson. She used all of her business and promotional skills and all her contacts who had an interest in the project to the advantage of the program. The event was a spectacular success and Katie was praised publicly for having surpassed all other chairpersons before her in the amount and number of contributions for the children served by the organization. She had reached her goal.

When Katie reached the end of her tenure as chairperson, she resigned her position rather than seeking reelection and decided to concentrate on promoting her own business interests. I believed she had the potential for success in anything she endeavored, considering her incredible performance as the first female chairperson of the board of an organization historically ruled by men. The board asked her to reconsider her resignation. She gracefully declined, bringing a fitting end to a heroic journey.

In Katie's Words:
In a television interview with a world famous singer and actress, an interviewer on *60 Minutes* (CBS) mentioned that the performer had once been in therapy for thirteen years. "Why so long?" the interviewer asked. The woman replied, "I'm a slow learner." I don't believe that this woman was a slow learner and I have no idea why she went into therapy. Perhaps she wanted a better quality of life. Everyone goes into therapy (unless they are so ordered by a judge) for their own personal reasons. I went into therapy because of the deaths of two very close people I dearly loved and I never had time to grieve. I was exhausted and, most of all, I was angry. I called for an appointment

and told my therapist that I needed a place to cry. When I got there, I sobbed and sobbed. It seemed I would never stop crying. When I was able to comprehend my painful situation, I learned that I had a lot of issues. I considered that if I wanted a better quality of life, I had better deal with those issues immediately.

The first thing I learned is that *I was angrier than I ever admitted.* I was more likely to sound off and to attack than I was to be patient and think before I acted. I learned that *I was a strong-willed woman.* I learned that, with a bit of personality realignment, *my reactive, feisty woman could learn to be more like Athena, the Warrior Goddess known for her intellect and wisdom.* I had always been attracted to owls (the bird of wisdom). One of the important characteristics of Athena was that, along with the owl, she had snakes surrounding her. I had always been afraid of snakes, but I reasoned that with a little attitude adjustment, I could rid myself of my "snake fear."

During the course of my therapy with Dr. Strick, I accepted a new leadership position to head a charity organization. This should have been an exciting and happy time for me. At the beginning of my term, it was not happy at all. I felt the all-male board of directors did all that they could to disrupt meetings and devalue my fundraising ideas in addition to being rude and unkind toward me. Instead of spending 100 percent of my time on my responsibilities, I was dealing with low masculine self-esteem, wounded egos, insecurity and jealousy. Talk about anger and disappointment! I was horrified. Why were they treating me this way?

During this terrible period, I had a dream. In my dream was a beautiful Snake with smooth white skin that sparkled with bold colored jewels and crystals. In my dream, this Snake was in control. She helped me change my life. She is my totem.

I learned to be more strategic in my communication with the board members and to write memos rather than speak directly to them. *I learned to fend off unwanted advances and to sidestep issues that were too hot to handle.* I had more confidence and could act with assertiveness when I had to deal with the many challenges in my new leadership position and elsewhere in my personal and professional life. My totem guided me to adjust both my personal and professional demeanor and that helped me to make major changes in my life, changes that I continue to use today.

I had other Snake totem dreams that helped me keep my balance through all the stresses I was experiencing. They shielded me when I was maneuvering and negotiating my way through responsibilities and attempting to achieve my goals. *I have learned patience*, but patience is still a work in progress for me. I still work on trust issues that were a challenge all through my life. *I learned that I could be in harmony with the masculine in myself and in the world. I learned to accept my soft, intuitive, feminine self* and that female friends can and do nurture each other. *I learned that being alone is solitude*, not necessarily loneliness.

I recognize that *I am responsible for myself now* and that I am blessed with health and a wealth of opportunities for an abundant life. I recognize that there always will be rough patches along the path of life and that whenever I lose sight of my proper path I can use therapy to right my course.

6.

Job Stress

Nicole, a woman with brown, shoulder-length, wavy hair attractively framing her face, was thirty-one years old when she arrived for therapy with me. Her chestnut eyes were glossy with tears not yet shed but not able to be contained either. Nicole worked as a social worker in a large multi-discipline facility with a well-defined hierarchy of power. Among the concerns she presented for discussion was a hostile work environment. She explained to me that her peers were critical of her and, at times, belittling. Worst of all, she felt that they tended to ignore her despite her best efforts to perform her duties conscientiously. In fact, her conscientious manner appeared to be a sore spot with other staff members who did not agree with her definition of patient care. Nicole was a trained and credentialed mental health counselor before she elected to study and earn an advanced degree in social work. She believed that the welfare of the patient was paramount and that all efforts should be expended to meet the expectations of the patient and the governing bodies of the healthcare industry. She experienced much resistance to this notion from her peers.

However, Nicole did experience a positive work relationship in terms of communication with her supervisor, but she came to learn that these communications did not reflect management's regard for her when it came to promotions. Although she was assigned more detailed and demanding work, she was not offered the pay increases that normally accompany a promotion, because she did not get a promotion. She only received a more intense workload. While credit for a job well done was often given to her by way of spoken word and responsibilities were added to her job duties, management did not follow up with pay increases. More than once, Nicole was not considered for a promotion versus another employee who had been with the firm a shorter time and whose level of expertise fell well below that which Nicole brought to the job.

Nicole told me she felt helpless to remedy the situations that caused other staff members to be angry and mean-spirited toward her. She felt that she could not confront management regarding her expectations, given the quality and quantity of her performance at work, for fear of being terminated. She was expected to perform her duties in a timely manner and, if need be, go beyond the requirements of her job. At the same time, her peers resented her for complying with the job requirements set out by management.

Another major problem Nicole was facing was the deterioration of her marriage of fewer than six years. That she would eventually become divorced was an especially stressful situation since she would be the first to be divorced in her very traditional family.

Nicole was the oldest child in her family. She had three sisters and five brothers. She was especially close to her sisters and brothers and relied on them for support. Nicole's father and mother were both deceased, her mother being the most recent parent to die. As a child, Nicole and her siblings were subjected to emotional and physical abuse from an early age. Her father was an addict and relied on drugs to get through each day. He was a quiet man and a steady provider for his family, but he was also under the domination of Nicole's mother.

While the family was not destitute, Nicole felt that they lived on the edge of poverty. Her father was not available emotionally or physically. Her mother's response to her husband's emotional distancing and his dependence on drugs was anger, which she readily displaced onto the children. Punishment was swift and unrelenting for any wrongdoing, perceived or real.

Reflecting on her childhood, Nicole could not recall ever seeing her mother laugh. She remembered the numerous meals her mother cooked and the formidable piles of laundry that accumulated each week. Somehow, her mother accomplished all there was to do in a day, but she was reactive and emotionally unavailable. Consequently, in response to the absence of emotional support, the children formed a strong bond and leaned on one another for support. Nicole felt it was her responsibility to attend to the family's needs. She was especially protective of her brothers and sisters and took seriously the self-imposed task of caring for her younger siblings.

When Nicole was eighteen years of age, her father became ill and died within a year. She grieved for his loss even though she had never realized a close and loving relationship with him. His death made life more difficult for the family, especially economically. They were a cohesive family and as the children began to earn money, they all contributed to the household and the family remained intact. When Nicole's mother realized that the family could and would survive the loss of her husband's income, she began to relax and seemed to be more content than ever before in Nicole's memory. Nicole found herself trusting her mother and managed to form a closer relationship with her in the years before her death.

When Nicole was twenty-five years old, her mother suffered a massive aneurism. Nicole sensed the gravity of the situation and lobbied on her mother's behalf to have her admitted to a hospital in the most efficient manner possible. She monitored the situation and intuitively felt that surgery was indicated immediately upon admission. Nicole's input was rebuffed by the doctors in charge her mother's care.

After several days of discussion and testing, surgery was indicated. Her heroic effort to save her mother's life was unsuccessful and Nicole's mother died before the surgery could be completed.

Nicole harbored bitter resentment and anger toward the medical team attending to her mother and placed the blame for her death on them for their failure to act in a timely manner. She felt betrayed by the medical profession and was unforgiving of them.

The family rallied after her mother's death, but soon cohesion suffered. Brothers and sisters became more distant, despite the fact that Nicole spent much effort trying to hold the family together. To complicate matters, Nicole had not yet made peace with her lack of relationship with her father nor had she made peace with his untimely death. It was evident that the grief process was not yet resolved, even though her mother was deceased for six years and her father for thirteen years prior to the day she decided to seek therapy with me.

Nicole married a popular political analyst when she was twenty-five years of age. Her husband was considerably older than she. Initially, he gave the impression that he enjoyed being active and involved socially and appeared to be well received among his peers. His job benefits included travel to exotic places and she was invited to join him on his many journeys to the far corners of the world. Nicole felt that she had made the ideal choice in choosing a husband and was, at first, content in the marriage.

To her sorrow, their private and social life began to deteriorate very soon after they were married. Instead of communicating with her at the end of the day, he retreated to his computer workstation and was involved with it until it was time to retire. He preferred darkness to light and insisted that the home be dimly lit when he was there. To object or to quarrel with him was of no avail since he would not respond to her concerns. Nicole's dismay at this turn of events was so intense that her husband ultimately agreed to meet with a therapist in an attempt to mend the growing rift between them. He soon determined that he was not in need of help and terminated marital therapy.

In desperation, Nicole proposed individual therapy but he refused and she suggested that a temporary separation could possibly help.

While he did not strongly object to separation, he vowed that he would not help in any way if she followed through with her intention to separate. Nicole knew that she could not tolerate the tension that, by now, was constant in the home. She felt caught between her role as wife and her need to be free of the constricting bonds of her marriage. In our discussion, she often referred to her parents' marriage and their decision to keep the family intact. Nicole felt guilty, because she could not do the same in her marriage.

Nonetheless, after much discussion and soul searching, she forged ahead to establish her own home. This decision proved to be economically disastrous for her and Nicole realized that she had to begin legal proceedings for spousal support at the least. She knew that she would eventually file for divorce. What she did not know was that it would take many years before the divorce settlement was resolved. She learned that her husband did not concede easily to sharing the gains they had made during their marriage. She was intimidated by him and his position and needed much encouragement to attend to the process of legal separation, divorce and the ultimate resolution of fair and equitable distribution of their assets. At the same time, Nicole felt sympathy for her husband. His childhood had not been much better than hers and she could readily identify with his pain to the extent that it sometimes made her weep. She was caught between her sympathy for her husband and her need for freedom from the constraints of her marriage.

Like Nicole, her husband was subjected to abuse as a child and his family lived on the edge of poverty. He vowed to prepare for himself a place in the world of politics and leave behind the tawdry remnants of his childhood. His goal was to be recognized as an expert in his field and wealthy enough that he would never fear for his survival again. Considering his experience of being deprived, one can understand his determination to hold onto the monies he earned. This battle for equality would not be easy for Nicole.

At the time she entered into therapy, Nicole was burdened with an overabundance of problems: grief, despair, helplessness, hopelessness and fear of loss on many levels—family, marriage, serious problems with her job, displacement and economic instability. *Where to start?* I wondered. In true Jungian tradition, the logical place to start was with the dream and to allow Nicole's journey to unfold by way of that dream. So we began our therapy:

> I am at an exhibition hall with separate booths. One booth has a bed in it. Father and daughter and two women are on the side, questioning each other about the body on the bed. The body is that of a woman. Her face is covered. She has been murdered. The women are being questioned by the district attorney. The men in suits believe me to be a psychic. A male friend walks by and then he stays right outside the room. Trapped in the room with the body and the men, I am frightened of my friend and of the three men. I feel certain that my friend is the murderer. When questioned by the district attorney, one of the women challenges the description of the victim. She is not small and blonde. On the contrary, she is big with dark hair. The district attorney is unrelenting in his insistence on the truth. I wake up terrorized. I feel that there is someone in the room.

It is not uncommon for the first dream to be very revealing. It is almost as though a dam breaks in the mind and it allows the contents that have been stored away for many years to be revealed to the dreamer. Once the content of the dream is made conscious, it can never go back into oblivion.

This dream touched on many areas of Nicole's life and was rich in imagery. Recalling that the initial motivating factor for entering therapy was the troubling situation in her workplace, the action in the dream supported Nicole's feeling of being disempowered (she cannot leave the room). Nicole was essentially as disempowered in the dream as she was in her work environment. The message in the dream was as conflicted as the message in the workplace. In the dream, she had special powers. In the workplace, she was told that she was "special." Nonetheless, she had no input in the process of making decisions regarding her staff, work assignments or any other matters that she encountered in the course of a day's work. She felt she was a puppet with no credibility with her staff or management. Identifying with the woman who had been murdered, Nicole felt that she was immobilized and had few resources to devote to problem solving in the workplace, even if she knew which way to turn.

I explored with her how the authority of the men in the dream could not be mistaken. Nicole compared it to the authority of her mother and management at her job. She described her mother as dictatorial and unrelenting. I asked Nicole to describe her own management style with her staff. When she demonstrated how she handled a staff problem, she was surprised at how much she sounded like her mother. Even though we may object to this manner of parenting, we can unconsciously develop the same style of interacting with others who are subject to our authority. "Now we know why your staff is angry with you," I observed.

Nicole did not absolve herself from punishment. When negative work or family situations presented themselves, she was all too ready to accept the blame. Nicole was in a tough position.

As her therapist I explained that there are two sides to everything: "We have the capacity to think clearly, as in managing our finances, and to have feelings of emotion, as in anger, excitement, fear, etc. These are opposites. We can choose to *act* or *react*." Nicole's work situation required *thinking through* the problems, developing a plan and executing the plan. To act in anger or passion was not being well received, as Nicole was learning.

The "father" portion of the dream actually represented her childhood experience with her father. In the family, her father was overshadowed and dominated by her mother and had no real input in decision making or childrearing. Even when the children were severely punished or reprimanded in his presence, he was silent and accepting of this situation, although his interactions with them were loving and positive. His escape was through drugs and work, leaving the children to cope with the situation without benefit of his protection (beyond providing for them financially).

The "murdered woman" described as "big with dark hair" was a fair description of Nicole. Seeing herself as "murdered" is a chilling sight. However, Nicole felt no particular concerns, with the exception that she felt just as immobilized as the murdered woman in the dream. To assign the first stirrings of mortality to this young, vibrant woman was unthinkable, yet the image was troublesome.

Our first task in therapy, at Nicole's request, was to address her problems in the workplace. Nicole's supervisors highly recommended but did not require team meetings. Nicole, pleading that she had too much to do and too little time, often cancelled team meetings in favor of e-mails to her staff. This kept her distanced from them and she had little personal contact with them, with the exception of complaints. At times, irate staff members bypassed her and went directly to management to voice their concerns. Her superiors called her in to address the complaints and/or problems. Nicole's response was to be defensive, complaining of the extra work requirements placed upon her by management. She felt caught up in an endless round of striving to meet the goals set for her and defending herself for her efforts. Supervisor and staff interactions were brief, with no room for argument or disagreement.

As Nicole and I explored patterns of communication, Nicole was able, through role-playing actual events in the workplace, to soften her tone and address problems in a manner that was more acceptable to her staff. She agreed to schedule regular team meetings, providing her staff with the opportunity to voice their opinions regarding work procedures. With practice, Nicole's attitude began to change and communication with her staff became easier. She learned to be more attentive and tactful, lending some relief to the work environment.

Her improved level of comfort did not extend to interactions with her superiors and Nicole continued to feel angry and fearful in any situation involving her supervisor. Somewhere between despair and hopefulness, Nicole's dreams continued and she shared:

> I am in a hospital. They put a patient on the table and leave the room and ignore him. I get disgusted with the nurse and minister to him. Alarms are going off and my mom is in a bed. It is upside down and someone is doing compressions on her. I look again and it is not my mom. It is a baby boy and someone is exercising his legs. The baby laughs.

The setting of this dream took Nicole back to her mother's death in the hospital. The action in the dream was a replay of the events surrounding her mother's death. Even six years later "alarms go off." It was as though it were happening all over again. Her grief had yet to be resolved, but there was hope: a laughing baby boy. The laughing baby made her want to cuddle something and babies are predictors of new beginnings. "This is good!" I encouraged Nicole.

Nicole's response to this dream was a softening that begged to be addressed. She decided that she needed a cat; in fact, she decided that she needed two cats so that they could keep each other company while she worked. It was wondrous to witness her loving attitude toward her "Kitty Girls," Dora and Nora. This event served as a springboard to begin to focus on loving and caring for herself; however, even as she was more effectively attending to her own needs and the needs of her staff, management continued to ignore her, no matter that her relationship with her staff and her productivity were improving.

Improvement was not the case in her marriage or in the family. Her family was unsettled and there was a large amount of conflict among her siblings. "It all seems too much to handle!" she exclaimed to me. Then she began to discuss life after death and past events that included her parents. The anniversary of her father's death was approaching and it was evident that she was still grieving for him. Her preoccupation with life after death was unusual for such a young woman, but anniversaries can generate such reflections. Her next dream left much room for thought about what all this activity around death meant:

> The dream takes place in the nineteenth century in Ireland or England. There are no colors in the dream. Everything is black and white. There is a woman in a long dress. She is very poor. With her is a girl and, in the room, there is a big wooden chest. He (the Man) is in Berlin. The Man is in a picture with a woman with long black hair. There is an old-fashioned lamp post that uses electric bulbs. The woman tells the girl to get a bulb, but she cannot get it. The Man has already given her the three bulbs he had. The woman walks ahead of the girl and leaves the room. A policeman reprimands the girl. He enters the house and is appalled at her poverty. He looks at her only possessions: a carved chest and chairs to match. A piece of her wooden chest is outside.

Nicole's experience of her life was poverty. As the oldest, she had to fend for herself and care for the younger children as well. She was subject to the absolute authority of her mother and so it was in the dream—only this time it was a policeman who had absolute authority. This inner male was not always as gracious as he turned out to be when he witnessed the desolation of her life. Nicole felt that she was never adequately cradled, so she did not know what it felt like. Even the few meager possessions she had (chest and chairs) were not intact, just as she felt that she was "broken." The box was the troublesome part of this dream. Wood has many meanings, including both the "cradle and the coffin."[1] On many occasions, Nicole voiced her thoughts of dying; even so, the symbolism of wood associated with a coffin did not resonate with her. After all, she was only in her thirties. Nevertheless, it seemed well worth noting. The extent to which Nicole was suffering with depression was serious. In spite of the burden of her life circumstances, she did not express any thoughts of suicide. Physically, she appeared to be in excellent health, working long hours and caring for her home and animals.

I found that Nicole kept a tight rein on her emotions. She despised any sign of weakness. Nonetheless, Nicole's defenses were beginning to melt down and she began to allow herself to express her anger and rage at her management, her family, her husband and the house that she and her husband occupied. She threw things she loved and demolished them vehemently. She hated "that house" with a passion. She had no input into the purchase of the house and felt that she could not live under the conditions imposed by her husband in a place that she could not bear to call a home. In her bid for freedom, she would receive no support from him and was faced with initiating legal action in order to address her spousal support concerns. She had little money to pay attorney fees. She was not comfortable with her job. She felt isolated from her family members, who were involved in their own problems. Her dreams became more violent. The rage she was experiencing was intense! Moreover, she was convinced that therapy was not helping at all and she considered terminating our sessions. A new dream she shared with me revealed much:

> It is nighttime. In a room, there is a man and woman. I am kneeling in between them. The man shoots me in the back of my head. I run away to a house, but the man who answers the door will not help me. He is afraid. He runs upstairs. Two children are there. A little girl shows me the way to get out. I run to another house. There is a glass door. The wall changes to glass with an iron grid. A

man is there. He will not close the iron grid. A crowd
comes in and I cannot escape.

Nicole had little patience to focus and logically attack her problems one at a time. This was the situation that caused the man in the
dream to be mean and nasty. He was the guide to cool-headed thinking
and planning. The intellectual part of Nicole was giving way to emotional bingeing. No matter where she turned, there was no escape. I
found it of some significance that Nicole was positioned between a
man and a woman. She felt that she was caught between her mother
and father and there was never an avenue of escape. After her parents'
deaths she continued to experience this dilemma with her family
members and husband. The family was having its own problems and
her husband was determined to undermine any gains she might make
to separate from him.

As our therapy progressed I found Nicole's reaction to the circumstances in her life was, in itself, very revealing. Nicole was prone
to denying any negative feelings in favor of maintaining the *good girl*
image (good daughter, good sister, good employee, good supervisor,
good wife, good friend, etc.). Just as her mother before her, she had
never learned safe expression of her anger. It was either denial or
extreme rage! She screamed and she cried until it seemed that there
were no more tears left.

In therapy, it is as though we start out on the bottom rung of a
ladder and gradually work our way up to the next rung and the next.
Oftentimes we slip back a rung. The task is to keep going on up the
ladder until finally we reach the top. In Nicole's case, her anger
exploded and she was out of control. Rage such as this is as though a
huge, dark cloud obscures all sense of reason. This experience for
Nicole was a good thing, because she came to realize that anger is neither
good nor bad. It simply is what it is. To experience anger is a human
experience. What is important is to learn safe expression of anger.
Nicole and I practiced how to express anger in a firm, no-nonsense

manner. This practice helped in the workplace but had no effect on her emotions at home. "I hate my life!" she said, exasperated.

Her dreams became even more intense and she endured a series of violent dreams in the next weeks. The themes of these dreams ran the range of her life experience: the abusive home situation, loss of her father and her mother and her failed marriage. Fear of death and death themes were constant, such as in this dream Nicole shared:

> I am in a car on the street. There is a man on the sidewalk. He is shabby and mean. I slide over to the door and try to raise the window of the car. He reaches in and cuts off the power. The window splits into two windows. He still tries to get into my car. I get mace. I have only two inches at the top. I spray the mace and get him. I coast downhill to my cousin's house. Just as I turn the corner, the man is there, lurking. I try to get my cousin to get through to the police. My brother walks in, but no one knows what to do.

I helped Nicole interpret the dream's symbolism: "The symbol of man in a dream is the call to let go of the emotional and to tend to solving problems in a reasonable, rational way." Nicole had been bingeing on emotions for a while and it was time to take heed of the danger of this behavior to her well-being. "You can't hide from your own psyche," I remarked. It was time to take action, but she wasn't ready yet.

One nightmarish dream followed another at a dizzying pace. Her sleep was fitful and disturbed. Her agitation was increasing and was more difficult to control, as seen in Nicole's next dream:

> I am outside in back of a house. The yard is sloped. There are small, sparse bushes. Beyond the yard, there are woods. It is an old neighborhood. My friend and her

baby are playing with the children there. I have a little
girl, about seven years old. No one likes her. She is a
wild child. I am angry, because they are being critical of
her. I can see inside her head like an autopsy. There is
blood in her head. I go back outside and yell at
everyone because of their criticism of my child.

It was as though all of Nicole's history was repeating itself in this
series of disturbing dreams. She recalled the feelings of desperation
in her childhood years. She always felt herself to be the last person to
be considered in the family. She was certain that no one really loved
her. She dared not express her anger for fear of retaliation from her
mother. (Keep in mind that although the conflicts with her mother
were resolved in her adult years, old wounds still emerged in the
unconscious and were apt to be relived over and over again until she
made peace with them.) In times of extreme stress as a child, she had
an intense reaction, screaming and throwing things, for which she was
soundly punished by her mother. The lessons of her childhood were
not easily forgotten or dispelled, so Nicole could do nothing yet to
loosen the grip her emotions had on her. It was as though a floodgate
gave way and Nicole was going under. She could not go on with discussion of her "little girl" and we dropped the subject for the moment.
In situations such as this, it is best not to go further into the dream
until the person is ready and able to accept and deal with the pain.

Nicole's marriage was anything but affirming. In fact, she was
experiencing deprivation and humiliation in both her marriage and
her job. Nicole had never learned to care for herself adequately and
was subject to the criticism of family, husband and management. It
was apparent that her anger had turned inward. She could only scream
at the world from her inner space at this point. She had, as far back as
she could recall, identified herself as the victim and she continued to
feel victimized in all areas of her life. One cannot even imagine the
effect of abuse on the psyche of the child until the dream exposes that

which lies deeply buried in the mind. In her next dream, the horror of her childhood was exposed:

> I am in Mother's house. Upstairs, outside the bedrooms, there are men throwing dead rats. Cats' legs are tied tail to tail. They put a miniature little house filled with roaches out. Some roaches come out, but other roaches stay in. There is tea with sludge for water. The tea is meant for my brother. It is winter and dark outside. Mother goes into a bedroom and then comes back out. My room is down the hall. I am afraid to go to bed. Mother is standing at the top of the stairs. I can see the roaches. They do not move.

Nicole's mother at the top of the stairs represented the all-powerful parent. She was so powerful that she even controlled the roaches. Everything vile and unclean was associated with her and the men in the dream were not friendly either. The only course to take was to respect the trauma that revealed itself in the dream and help Nicole to own it and to accept that she could not change history.

Nicole's depression was worsening and even though she resisted, I advised her that a course of antidepressants was in order. Nicole had a family history of depression. Her mother and two of her sisters were diagnosed and treated for depression. The idea is to resolve emotional problems with psychotherapy, but one has to take into account that genetics may be involved. She agreed to seek the advice of a medical doctor who specialized in natural remedies. She also agreed to take his advice if he felt that traditional remedies were more appropriate, given the nature of her depression and the length of time she had been depressed. She was so exhausted from the poor sleep time she had been experiencing. She certainly needed relief and some tender, loving care. Dreams being what they are, this next dream provided a measure of relief for her. Dreams of this nature are compensating for what the dreamer needs and does not have:

> I am in my mother's bedroom in the back of the house.
> My father is dying. I lean over him and say his name. He
> gets up and hugs me.

Nicole harbored bittersweet memories of her father. She knew his love for her was unmistakable, even though he could or would do nothing to protect her against her mother's wrath. She had always accepted his unconditional love with gratitude. She awoke feeling refreshed, secure in the knowledge of his love.

Nicole had a constant preoccupation with life after death. She spoke with me once again about being reunited with her parents. The themes of being killed and the preoccupation with death were disturbing to the point that I began to question whether I was sensing suicidal tendencies or some underlying medical problem. She looked healthy and said she felt physically well. She worked hard every day, tended to her cat family, kept in touch with friends and, with the exception of her psychological pain, gave the appearance of a healthy, functioning thirty-something woman. She denied any thoughts of suicide. On the contrary, she claimed to have great plans for the future. The next dream belies all of this:

> I am in a medieval, barren land. There is a man on top of
> a castle. He is dressed in black. A young girl appears on
> the land. She is a peasant. She calls out, "My father is
> king." She is happy to announce this to the man. He
> appears to be listening to her. From around the corner,
> an archer appears with a weapon. The man tells him to
> kill her. He shoots and she dies.

As our sessions continued Nicole realized that this was the theme of many of her dreams: death and dying. She felt that parts of herself had been killed off all her life, first by her mother, then her husband and management. It all seemed to converge and Nicole's sadness was so intense that she developed physical symptoms, particularly stomach pain. I advised her to seek the services of her medical doctor to rule out any serious internal problems that might be occurring, such as an ulcer. After a number of diagnostic tests, which were negative for any internal problems, her doctor assured her that she was in fine physical condition. Her doctor prescribed a different medication for her depression and, after a few weeks, she and I saw a noticeable difference in her mood and an improved ability to function in the workplace, but her stomach pain was not resolved. She felt very much like the peasant girl, defenseless and undefended. In the next dream, her dream compensated for the lack of love in her life:

> I am in the front passenger seat of a car. A man is in the driver's seat. I feel awkward. I reach out to touch the radio. He takes my hand, puts it on the seat and puts his hand on top of mine. His touch is very gentle.

Nicole relayed to me that she felt refreshed after this dream. With the combination of medication and therapy, her moods stabilized and she began to feel more settled. It was an opportune time to plan for her future. Conditions at work had not improved and she began to interview in earnest for other jobs within the same organization. She intended to make a lateral move, stay with the organization and thus not lose any of her benefits.

Nicole's credentials were so impressive that she was offered another position in just a few weeks. She submitted her resignation and was surprised at the reaction of her staff. They strongly opposed her leaving the facility and went so far as to petition management to offer her anything that would prevent her from leaving. Management made an offer, but Nicole refused and prepared herself to begin a new job almost immediately. To her surprise, her staff presented her with gifts and hosted a farewell party for her. Nicole was very moved by their kindness and recognition of her efforts. Tears flowed and hugs and kisses were abundant. She felt much more confident in herself and ready to begin the next chapter of her career. I hoped that her

dreams would reflect this amazing event, but her newest dream did
not rejoice with her:

> I am in a room with a family. There is a baby there, about
> two-and-one-half years old. It is my sister's baby. I go
> into another room. There is nothing but a commode
> there. A truck pulls up. Two men emerge wearing black
> surgical masks and T-shirts with skulls and bones
> imprinted on them. I grab the baby and hurry down a
> sloping hill in the back. I come to an alley and stay there.
> There is no phone to call the police. I see a bulletin
> board with Arabic and Egyptian writing. The sixth name
> is the name of the person who is missing. I leave the
> alley and go up the street with the baby.

Once again, I observed, Nicole faced the specter of death and a
desperate attempt at survival. This was the second appearance of a
baby in Nicole's dreams. This time, she was brave and was intent on
saving her own "baby" self from the intruders who invaded the house
she was visiting. It was a strange landscape she described in her quest
to save the baby and herself: an alley, a narrow, dark passageway,
almost paralleling the birth canal. In this passageway, she encountered
the Egyptian hieroglyphics and ancient Arabic text: sacred messages
that the ancients had left for those who travel there. Because she was
able to read the text, she knew and acknowledged that there was a
"missing person" and he or she was characterized by a specific number: six. The number six is associated with, among other things, "per-
fection and completion."[2] Completion means the end has come. The
task is done. That there was a missing person in the number six spot
was chilling. The idea of completion did not seem to fit with the events
of her life at the moment, but it could have been a sign of the future.

The other symbol in the dream—T-shirts with skulls and bones,
the traditional symbols of death—begged to be addressed. At thirty-
something, the idea of mortality did not come easily to mind. What

was important was that Nicole experienced it as a sign of hope that she would reach a state of harmony with herself and the world about her and she strived to make that happen as best she could.

Nicole went to work in her new position in the company as an entry-level manager with twelve supervisees on her team. This represented an increase in the number of subordinates from her previous job. She expected to be considered on a par with the other managers, so to speak.

Nicole was excited by the challenges of the new position. She had learned well how to interact positively and tactfully with her staff. Her staff's response to their new manager was typical of a changed situation: Some of her staff members were openly welcoming, while others were somewhat reserved. She persevered and was gradually earning the acceptance of the majority of her staff.

Diplomacy was not one of Nicole's strong points, especially when she was interacting with people in authority. To her dismay, Nicole felt that her assigned supervisor spoke in an abrupt manner suggestive of a bad-tempered, domineering woman who would tolerate no discussion on the subject of her opinions. Nicole simply could not apply her newfound knowledge to authority figures and she reacted with anger and resentment. She could not distinguish between helpful information and censure and her interpersonal relationship with her supervisor was deteriorating on a daily basis, just as it had in previous jobs.

While discussing her current problems with management, we discovered that the way Nicole responded to this newest supervisor was exactly the way she had acted with her mother when she was punished, criticized and scolded. While she had learned not to be critical and demanding with her staff to get the best possible performance from them, she could not accept criticism or even suggestions from anyone in authority. Every time she was in the presence of her supervisor, she became defensive and argumentative. She was not yet able to tell the difference between her mother and other authority figures.

Anger got the best of her and she was, once more, reliving her early experience with her mother. When this happens, our emotions control us and we cannot think clearly. The best way to address this problem is to recreate it in the therapy session and play it out just as the person remembers it. Nicole began to understand that she was caught up in old wounds and she tried very hard to listen to suggestions from her superiors without reacting. When we are not allowed to express ourselves as children, we cannot know how it feels to be confident. This next dream helped me and, subsequently as we explored it, Nicole to understand the serious wounding to her self-esteem:

> I am in Africa. I wear hospital "scrubs" (humble, practical, no-nonsense attire most commonly worn in hospitals and operating rooms). Others are wearing traditional dress of every color and design. Initially, everyone is outside. There is a young man there. He is my intended husband. I am afraid. I run uphill and he pursues me. He is smiling and laughing. Then I am inside a church. Those of us who are inside are considered to be of a lower class. The people are coming into my place. The man and I are upstairs in a room. There are all men in the room. I sense that they are dangerous. Then I see children. I am trying to round them up. I am especially intent on protecting a small boy.

We explored how the setting of the dream put Nicole in a tribal ceremony of great importance: a celebration, a wedding. This ceremony was important enough to inspire the guests to dress in their finest, except for her. She wore humble scrubs. She was running away from the men only to find herself in a church where, in the modern world, such ceremonies take place. Not so in the tribe. The custom of being married in a church was considered to be reserved for the "lower class." Nicole had never felt herself to be in the same class as others. Was there any place to run and be both safe and equal? Was there any place she could take her child-self and be safe? It did not appear to be so in the dream.

Such a scene suggested extremely low self-esteem to me. This was so because, in her mind, Nicole had not developed the self-worth she needed to fit in with the group. One of the dreadful outcomes of child abuse is low self-esteem. Nicole had no way to own her special, unique self, since her early experience of childhood was punishment, criticism from her mother and lack of emotional support from her father. Under these conditions, by the time Nicole was of school age and exposed to other children, she expected to be judged harshly. She was often the most judgmental toward herself.

As in many of her dreams, danger lurked. She knew the men were dangerous and that she must gather the children and run. Always running, but where was there safety except within herself? As long as she was driven to defend herself instead of observing, listening and learning, she was setting herself up for more of the same with her superiors. It was as though she was in a cycle of self-destruction. She needed to make a more committed investment in logical problem solving. Coping strategies start very early in childhood and the way we cope is generally well fixed by the time we are adults. Therapy is thus a whole new learning process. One of the goals of therapy is to learn new skills and learn them so well that there is no going back to the old way of being in the world: guarded and angry.

In the course of life events, psyche, karma or fate (whatever you want to call it) works in a way that forces us to encounter the same or similar problems over and over until we finally make resolution with them. Psyche will give us all the tools we need to change a situation and if we do not heed the call, she will give us a kick and continue to create similar situations—as many times as it takes.

Nicole and I role-played the interactions between her and her supervisor and repeated the same role-play with Nicole and her mother. This proved to be a great help in developing a more tolerant attitude toward her supervisor. While this was not the ultimate solution, she functioned on a more acceptable level.

Other events of special significance in Nicole's life happening concurrently were the separation, divorce and financial problems she was experiencing as a result of her decision to end her marriage. As her husband refused to help her, Nicole's rage increased. She had little control over her emotions and she allowed the bitterness and anger she felt to spill over into the workplace, further complicating her work situation. It didn't stop there! Nicole was angry and hostile with her attorney. She argued with the judge while she was trying to get the sympathy of the court. She felt victimized in all areas of her life.

The effect of these combined problems was devastating. She broke down in tears often and experienced long, sleepless nights. She felt weary and I found it evident that the antidepressant was no longer providing the relief she initially experienced. She agreed to a consultation with her medical doctor and was prescribed a different medication. Her mood improved. She was making small gains on a steady basis and that was exactly what we hoped would happen.

To help Nicole learn to communicate more effectively, I advised her to take a public speaking course. The course, which she completed, did wonders to teach her to focus on the subject at hand and, through training and example, keep a respectful distance between herself and everyone else in her life. The course proved to be valuable for interactions on a general level. She learned to tell the difference between the challenging events that were occurring in her new job and the stresses of her personal life. She learned not to confuse the two. For example, her supervisor was not her mother reincarnated.

With her husband it was a different story. In this one area, her rage could not be contained very well. He had money. Couldn't he share? He knew the marriage was a mistake. Nicole was angry and hurt. Through intensive role-play in our sessions, she was able to accept the challenge of attending to each situation with her head and not her emotions. She improved in her court appearances to the extent that she began to earn the sympathy of the judge hearing her case for spousal support. However, her frustration was almost unbearable.

Even though she could hold her own in court, privately she felt diminished and degraded and it showed in her next dream:

> There are a man and a woman in the scene. She is there, because she was kidnapped by a man. She is wearing a dress at first. She opens the door and crawls out on her stomach. Her clothes have changed to dark clothing and she wears a skirt. She runs through a wind tunnel. He is in pursuit of her. There are buildings and a parking platform. She comes to a corner. There is no way to get away. She says, "Well, are you going to kill me?" He replies: "No, not if we get along."

We discussed how this was a dream of her present situation. She was having problems controlling her emotions and her judgment was poor (such as quarreling with the judge). In the dreams of women, the man represents cool-headed logic and reason. To give in to emotion and lose control by indulging in and exposing feelings is to invite a nasty dream. Psyche demands balance and lets dreamers know it by way of the dream. Emotion has its place and reason has its place!

Nicole was successful in gaining the sympathy of the court. The judge ordered spousal support to begin retroactively from the date Nicole first filed for support. This was a relief for her and her mood improved tremendously. She had settled into her new position and was enthusiastic about her work. She was better able to put psychological distance between her supervisor and herself and all seemed to be going well. Staff relations were tolerable in some cases and excellent in others. The important thing was that she was able to distinguish between business and parental issues, so that if she was involved in discussion with a supervisor, she did not personalize the interaction. She reported to me that her sleep patterns were improving as well.

After all of the excitement and trauma of the trial, Nicole was feeling very lonely and isolated. Friends whom she had abandoned

during the time of her serious depression were distant and not available. She especially missed her close relationship with her family. She
alternated between anger and pain and her dreams began to show
signs of serious preoccupation with the death of her mother. She
blamed herself for not being able to convince the doctors to act
quickly. Her dream reflected her frustration:

> I am in a basement room. Mother is sickly and bloated.
> A man comes in and picks her up and runs into the next
> room. I chase him. He is crouching over a sewer. Mother
> is under water. I reach in and get her out. I hug her. I am
> so angry! I tell him that he isn't permitted to touch her.

The whole scene of her mother's illness and death seemed to
have exploded in her mind. The dream had a profound effect on her
mood and her cooperation in therapy. It was as if she transferred all
the rage she held to the therapy experience.

At this point, Nicole refused to discuss anything with me. She
became passive in our therapy sessions. She offered little or no communication and sat tight-lipped and unavailable from beginning to end
of each session. Nonetheless, she kept all of her appointments and
doggedly stayed with her program of silence. She was, in fact, demon-
strating her inner strength and challenging my authority just as she
had with her mother.

In this situation, I find it is best to wait it out. It is not advisable
to interfere with the process. I have found that no meaningful communication occurs when a therapist imposes her thoughts or opinions
on a client when this is occurring. Silence can be therapeutic. The
problem resolves itself eventually and the experience becomes meaningful. The insights gained meanwhile are important. And so it was
with Nicole. One day, she just took up where she left off and the work
of therapy continued.

As Nicole became more engaged in her life on many fronts, work and divorce proceedings were at the forefront. She was, at the same time, resentful of the loss of her feeling of *nothingness*. Nothingness, for Nicole, represented her dance between wanting to live or die. When she was electing to give in and give up, she entered into a state of emotional detachment and she felt nothing. At least she was not hurting, however sorrowful her situation. But she had chosen life and that meant being engaged, even though it was so difficult at times. Her time-out from the therapeutic work was a rest. I felt reassured that she did not rest to the point that she skipped her weekly sessions, for that, in itself, was a statement of her dedication to healing.

In the case of childhood abuse, I conveyed to her, the casualty is the loss of childhood. Deep inside the mind there exists an inner child. Nicole was acutely aware of the wounded child she harbored some-where in her mind. In another dream of the inner child (it seemed that this child would not be ignored) they became acquainted. The dream had no story, only an image. She described this dream image in more detail than she had in the previous image of the lost and abused child:

> Cara is seven years old. She has long, black, stringy hair.
> She is skinny, quiet and melancholy. She is not allowed out.

This image took Nicole back to the original pain of childhood. This child was not playful or creative. Her sparkle had been tarnished by the cruelty of her mother's anger, the family situation, the poverty and the inability of her father to help. In a family of many children, she was lost in the crowd. She was skinny and her hair was stringy. There was no one to see to her nourishment and care. Not only was she abandoned, but also she was not "allowed out." She was a prisoner of life and circumstance.

What a fantastic breakthrough this is! I thought. *Now Nicole can actively care for her own wounds. She is charged with nurturing her own child self.* Nicole and I held many significant discussions regarding Cara's care. I asked Nicole to whom she should delegate the care of this child. She firmly refused to put her into the care of anyone else. However, she did not know how she was supposed to parent this child, so she declined the task herself, leaving Cara motherless again. Even though she doubted her ability to parent anything, I explored with her that she was, in fact, mothering her cats every day. After pointing this out to her I posed the question, "Are you really a mother cat in disguise?" When I jokingly asked her this she burst out with a hearty laugh. The tension and fear appeared to lighten from that point on. She was visibly more relaxed and, with some apprehension, agreed to the task of nurturing her child self.

One of the first goals I gave Nicole was to be kinder to herself. She had always wanted to visit the land of her ancestors and meet members of her family who still resided there. She was able to negotiate this journey with a family member and it was a successful experience. Her relatives were delighted to have them as guests and made them welcome. She returned happy and relaxed. Cara, whom she allowed to "go" with her, also had a great time. Nicole was acutely conscious of her new charge, her very own baby Cara, and kept her in consciousness. For example, going to market was an adventure to be shared with her and Nicole included her in all the fun things that she felt able to engage in at the time, especially on Christmas Day when the entire family joined together, gaily dressed in holiday costumes: Santa Claus, elves, reindeer and angels. This was a happy time for Nicole.

Nicole was content in her new job and had mastered the difficult task for which she was hired. Except for normal ups and downs, all was going well. She had learned to maintain her own space. She was able to separate herself from her supervisor's outbursts, manner of speaking and giving orders. She accepted that her supervisor's method of communication and giving direction was unique to her supervisor. She was not taking everything personally. I noticed she smiled a lot those days.

As time passed, Nicole continued to do well in her work situation and she was proud of the way she was handling assignments and staff problems. Her productivity was excellent. She was, however, working sometimes sixty hours each week. She was not reimbursed for overtime but reasoned that, since she did not have children, she could devote more hours to her job. She had no social life except for family events. She also was very tired most of the time and while she looked healthy enough, she was having trouble remaining calm in difficult situations. Nevertheless, when I suggested cutting back to a forty-hour workweek, she said absolutely no. She felt that she had to prove to management that she was capable of excelling on the job. Nothing could dissuade her from her goal: to be the best manager her organization ever had, even though she was feeling overwhelmed and weary. Her next dream had chilling implications:

> I am in a room with a scrubs top on. I am cleaning the room but I am breathing hard from exhaustion. There is a police officer there and he is concerned that I am so tired. I lie down on a bed and the officer is on the other side of the bed. Kitty Girl Dora is lying lengthwise on the bed. She is so warm. The police office comes around to my side of the bed and rubs corn starch on my breast. He gently kisses me.

"Remember, the dream speaks in symbols!" I reminded Nicole. But we needed to explore just what her dream meant. Was this just a nice man soothing Nicole, because she was so tired? I explained it was quite the contrary: Tribal societies revere corn as the grain of life but, as in nature, in the fall of the year they are "burned and reborn as the spring."[3] This is the law of nature: death and rebirth, I revealed. I analyzed her dream. In the manner that Nicole described it, the focus on her breasts did not seem to me to suggest sexual contact; it was more suggestive of a healing, soothing touch. The kiss was likewise more compassionate than sensual. I told her that kisses can also mean the kiss of death. Once again, the dream ego presented an allegory of death, this time with the promise of rebirth.

Nicole's unusual extreme exhaustion, I believed, could be the effect of her sixty-hour workweeks plus caring for her home and cats. She was also taking antidepressants and one of the side effects of such drugs could be feeling tired. However, I was not willing to theorize. Once again, I advised Nicole to get a medical checkup to determine the state of her health and also to evaluate her medications. Her doctor advised that she only needed a medication adjustment. She agreed with this diagnosis and followed through with the recommended medications. She still insisted that she would not consider cutting back on her hours at work. This was where she was feeling valuable and empowered, a heady feeling. Her medical advisors did not investigate further since no specific symptoms were able to be identified.

Her mood improved after her medical checkups and medication adjustments. All appeared to be going better. She developed a meaningful relationship with a friend, a mother of a young child, and she delighted in bringing surprises for the woman's little son when she visited. In these visits Nicole reported to me she found herself playing at the level of the child and these playtimes were precious. Nicole allowed Cara, her child self, to play, too.

Meanwhile, wonderful things were happening in Nicole's family. One of her brothers was getting married and the sisters were attendants at this momentous event. Nicole and her sisters reveled in the fun of choosing dresses and hairstyles. She was happy and the dream she told me about reflected this feeling:

> Two men and I are mountain climbing. I do very well and make it to the top of the mountain first. I am triumphant!

This was a blessed and happy time for Nicole. Her dream reflected her good spirits and sense of accomplishment with her family and her job and an openness to life for the first time. She was playful with the men in her dream about mountain climbing, even though she competed with them. They were not shooting her in the head or being nasty or violent as in previous dreams. I realized she had come a long way since the early days of her therapy with me.

When one suffers a serious depression as Nicole did, giving up long and cherished friendships is quite common during such periods. Now, she had the need to have friends in her life again. She reunited with her best friend since childhood and felt supported and fulfilled. She felt so confident in herself that she consented to a vacation trip with her estranged husband. On this journey, she could sense his vulnerability and actually felt compassion for him for the first time in many years. The trip was successful and she felt some remorse at the prospect of ending her marriage but did not want to reunite with him because of her serious marital problems. However, Nicole now felt relaxed and at peace with herself and with the world.

As our therapy progressed Nicole's social life expanded and she met a man who was attracted to her. She enjoyed his company and life was fun again, even though her divorce had not yet been finalized. They were both mature and understood the situation, so they were cautious in their expectations. They agreed to be friends.

Then Nicole found out her temporary living arrangements were no longer available. She still depended on her husband to help with any extraordinary expenses. She asked her family to help her purchase a home of her own and a car that she would feel safe driving. They agreed to do both. A sibling was listed as joint owner of the property to shield her from having to declare sole ownership in any court proceedings. Soon she found a suitable home and felt excited about her new life. Members of her family helped renovate the house to her specifications at cost. Nicole expressed her happiness and excitement about moving with her cats to her new home. Life was looking good, despite the specter of divorce and financial uncertainty.

However, while these were happy times, they were also stressful. Nicole's petition for divorce was filed, but the legal process takes time.

She felt the pace was maddeningly slow. Nicole began using food for comfort. She gained a considerable amount of weight, because no matter how much she ate she still felt hungry and had little energy. "I feel paralyzed, unable to move," she explained to me. She was barely functioning outside of work. Often, as people face difficult situations they resort to unhealthy or even addictive means of coping. So it was with Nicole at this critical time in her life.

Where she felt the most in control was in the workplace. She never dreamed that her position could or would be eliminated, but it was and she lost her job. She was no longer in charge of the department. Immediately Nicole set out to find another position. She would not accept this insult, this put-down, once again; not ever, she vowed.

Nicole's history was such that she came to any new position well credentialed. That she was able to maintain her leadership role with dignity in her department was a testament to her growth and development. She had moved well beyond the acting-out behaviors she previously demonstrated whenever she was disappointed. She researched new positions and was quickly hired by another facility.

While dealing with this trauma in her private life and change in her work situation in quick succession, Nicole began to experience intense pain that she had never had before. She developed a sinus infection and flu-like symptoms. Also, she had arthritis-type pain and ear problems. Her body did not respond well to treatment and was very slow to heal.

It was under these conditions that Nicole began a new job. Despite feeling ill, she invested the time and effort to learn the new system, train a new staff and position herself for advancement. Very soon, however, she realized that the demands of her new job were unreasonable and she quietly went about applying and interviewing for other positions. She reasoned that she would not let herself feel like a failure, because this job had turned out to be overwhelming. She also toyed with the idea of earning a graduate degree in business.

It was at this point she found a dreaded lump in her breast. "Now we know what the dreams were telling me about," she said sadly. "All these months, cancer was developing." One could suspect that her dreams had been indicating that she had a serious, life-threatening problem, even pointing to the location of the cancer (the corn starch rub on her breast). By the time she found the lump, it was significant and her doctors felt she needed radical surgery. She submitted to surgery and survived the mastectomy very well. Afterward, she looked forward to the reconstruction process.

During her health crisis, Nicole was surprised at the support that she received from her new staff and her superiors, considering that she had been hired just a short time before her surgery. Though her salary was decreased while she was on leave, she planned to resume her duties as soon as she could, post-surgery. She engaged a specialist in alternative medicine and added natural remedies to the traditional methods of combating the cancer. Together, the specialists worked as a team with her traditional physicians to obtain the optimal level of healing and recovery.

Even as she faced chemotherapy, her mood was positive. She refused to allow herself to experience the agony of losing her hair a little at a time, so she had her hair stylist shave all her hair at once, in her words, "to get it over with." She purchased very attractive, multi-colored head cover-ups that were engaging and fun. She got a large supply to keep her choices interesting. She refused to give up on therapy with me and kept as many of our appointments as she could, depending on how ill she was feeling on any given day.

Nicole had filed for additional spousal support given the decrease in her salary and she was ordered to appear in court to testify. The court had little tolerance for any more delays. Though she was going through cancer and chemotherapy the court did not absolve her of appearing and somehow she managed to go to court and testify on her own behalf. I tried to convey how much I admired her fortitude and to give my support. In my view, her resolve was unwavering and the strength of this woman, who experienced herself as weak all of

her life, was remarkable. She smiled when I brought this to her attention and thanked me for my concern but indicated she had found new
strength within herself.

Unfortunately, Nicole's cancer had spread and she developed
lymphoma. More surgery was scheduled even though her immune
system was seriously challenged. She also continued to work as many
days as she could, given the situation. Her staff did as much as they
could to support her by taking on added work. Both her staff and
supervisors were involved and supportive of her. After she gained
strength and recovered, Nicole proceeded with breast replacement
surgery. The effect on her overall well-being was twofold: She was
relieved to feel attractive again but exhausted from the ordeal.

Soon, tests indicated that the cancer was in remission. Nicole
told me she still felt an underlying dread that more of the cancer was
threatening and waiting. She could not shake the feeling. Then Carlin,
a dear friend, was diagnosed with breast cancer that quickly spread to
her lungs. Carlin was considered to be terminally ill. Having cancer
herself, Nicole identified with Carlin and felt much grief as her friend
grew more and more ill. It took much support and counseling to help
Nicole to separate herself from Carlin's fatal illness.

A few months later, Nicole's family invited her on a trip abroad.
Her own chemotherapy was completed and her hair was growing
again. She had a beautician cut and style her hair in a short, attractive
style and off she went to Europe. She returned happy but weary. She
had developed bronchitis and flu-like symptoms, which were difficult
to resolve. She was able to heal from the latest bout of illness, but she
still felt exhausted. Divorce proceedings continued and she doggedly
met all the requirements set forth by the court. Her financial future
was at stake and she never gave up on that!

Unfortunately, after a few months, more lesions were found in
addition to her developing a serious reaction to a vine that she
attempted to cut back in her yard. Her doctor administered massive

doses of steroids, further compromising her immune system. Nicole's sleep was disturbed and she was tearful and despondent in our sessions together. Her doctors changed her medications to help control the developing depression symptoms and to aid in sleep. In addition, her doctors ordered a scan. She was frightened of the possible outcome of this latest investigation into the progress of the cancer. Her fears were not unfounded: the cancer had invaded her left lung.

Her treatment team recommended lung surgery and chemo-therapy. They felt these needed to be the next step in attempting to destroy the invading cells. As Nicole prepared herself for the ordeal, she had a dream concerning her illness:

> Mother is ill. I am distraught. She is walking ahead of
> me. I am calling out to her. She turns around but keeps
> walking. She looks very weak.

Nicole's first impression of this dream was the observation that her mother seemed to appear in her dreams when she was in serious trouble. Nicole was worried by the image of her mother in this dream. It appeared, from the dream image of her mother as ill and walking ahead of her, that there was an element of her own death to consider. She did not recall whether she followed her mother, only that the dream ended with her mother walking away from her. It appeared that Nicole's time had not yet come, notwithstanding the spread of her cancer. Nicole was upset and uneasy about this dream. Neverthe-less, she declared: "I am not ready to give up. I just started this amazing job and I am not going to fail this time."

I increased her therapy sessions from once a week to twice a week when she could manage them and I advised her to call me at any hour, if need be, for support. Nicole had always been faithful to her therapy and this time in her life was no exception. In fact, she felt the need for therapy to be even greater than when she had been relatively healthy. She told me she welcomed the comfort of the therapy room and I understood why when she shared her next dream with me:

> I am in the ocean, floating on huge waves.

We explored how Nicole felt that she had no control over her life anymore. The court system would determine her financial future, her body was being cut away from her due to the cancer and she felt weak and powerless to stop the chain of events, but nevertheless she was not ready to give in or give up.

Unfortunately, because she was so young and still producing the normal amount of estrogen for a woman her age, her medical team felt that the production of estrogen in her body was detrimental to the control of the cancer's spread. So her treatment team's recommended procedure was to perform a total hysterectomy to discourage estrogen production. She joked with me that she would not be having babies anyway; besides, she had enough to do to care for her Kitty Girls. Her next shared dream illustrated the powerlessness that she was feeling:

> I am in a dangerous place. They're shooting poison
> darts at me. I cannot escape.

This dream reflected the dread of more surgery and chemotherapy. Nicole understood that although she would feel ill from them, the chemicals killed the cancer cells, but that was of little comfort to her while she was experiencing the process. The good news was that her family was ever vigilant and dedicated to her care. She was amazed at this, because she had experienced so little nurturance in her life that to receive any caring at all seemed like a miracle. Though she appreciated their care, the pain of her condition as well as the pain of her divorce occupied her dreams:

> I am driving a car. I lose control and the car goes off the
> side of a bridge. I am not hurt. I look down and see a
> river monster, black in color. The river bed has dried up.

The monster turns into dead children. The river bed is littered with large, chunky pieces of jewelry. I pick some of the jewelry up. I feel that it is bad luck to take it and I leave it there.

During the course of her marriage, Nicole had acquired many pieces of jewelry of significant value. In the court proceedings, the jewelry was considered to be joint property and was being assessed by an independent expert. She said to me, "My marriage is ashes. Any potential that was ever possible is dead now, as dead as the children in this dream." Nicole felt strongly that to keep the jewelry would, in some way, harm her. She petitioned the court to award her the monetary value of the jewelry. The court decided in her favor and she felt tremendous relief that she did not "take the jewelry." This was an act of letting go of the old and starting anew.

I felt Nicole was now the mistress of flexibility. Starting over had become an ordinary event in her life. She approached each start-over point as a new adventure and spent little time grieving over material things such as the loss of her jewelry. There were so many more important matters to which to attend. The whole thing felt like a nuisance. Once the court ruled in her favor, she put it behind her and concentrated on healing. She felt a sense of relief that the hysterectomy was completed but, as expected, she began to experience the classic signs of menopause: hot flashes that caused sleep disturbance and gross discomfort. Nonetheless, she performed her work duties and met the requirements for number of days worked to continue to earn benefits and support herself.

Then one day she was asked to report to the office of the president. With a dreadful feeling in the pit of her stomach, she entered the room, fully expecting to be terminated. Instead, the president advised her that she was being promoted to the position of director of social services with a significant raise in pay. Nicole accepted the position with pride and vowed to give the job her best effort. Plans were dancing in her head and when she told me what had occurred I found her enthusiasm a joy to see!

She performed in the capacity of director for two years before the cancer spread to other organs. From this point, progression of the cancer was rapid and her dream revealed what was impending:

> I am bringing a gift to my therapist. I try to get off the elevator on the third floor. There is a security door. I cannot find the name on the door. A woman and a couple come in and the woman is able to get me in. I am in a conference room. There are windows on the other side of the room. The view is very pretty. Other couples are there. There is food for everyone.

I analyzed that the dream revealed Nicole was weakening and needed the assistance of others to "find the right door." We spoke of how the dream seemed to foretell the end of her self-sufficiency. She would soon have to rely on help from others. She was well fortified and in the dream she had the gift of food. Food offers strength and nourishment. She was ready now to share and be involved. She decided not to isolate herself and withdraw into her sadness, even though her best efforts at survival did not appear to have been successful. Even so, she could enjoy the view from the vantage point of the dream room high above the ground. The gift she bore was the gift of gratitude. The physical properties of the dream's location (on an upper floor with windows on the other side) were actual descriptions of the physical space of my office. In our therapy sessions we discussed how Nicole could look out and survey the landscape of her life. Most importantly, she had risen above it all.

For several months, all was quiet. Nicole and her support team of physicians and advisors did all they could to prevent the cancer's spread to other parts of her body. She was faithful to her oncologist's recommendations, but she had underlying feelings of anxiety. She dreamed several turbulent dreams in quick succession, some on the same night:

> A nude woman is in bed, bound. A vampire is drinking the blood from her wrist. Under the sheet, a cup of blood is there to be drunk later. A man fights off the vampire and will not let him drink.

We spoke of how the significance of this image was unmistakable. She was overcome by the "evil one." This was a horrific image of death and yet there was also a hero. Nicole felt that her time had not yet come. She loved her work and was doing well. Her treatments seemed to be working and no new physical problems had developed with the exception of more fatigue. She was feeling very tired but still hopeful. However, her dreams were fitful:

> A psychiatrist is rubbing my chest and upper back with lotion. I am uneasy. He is touching the area of the cancer.

Once again, the focus was on her chest, as it was in the dream of corn starch on her breast; a sign of what was to come. The attention, the balm and the healing hands of the gentle man, while not unpleasant, frightened her. Nicole felt that the touch was meant to soothe and heal as opposed to sexual energy. "Why now?" she questioned. "We do not know why now," I answered. Although she said there were no new symptoms, I advised her, because of her own anxiety displayed in her dreams, to ask her physician to recheck all her systems thoroughly. Then in her next dream her totem made itself known. It was the Serpent, a powerful symbol of death, renewal and resurrection:

> I am standing, holding a snake. We are looking at each other. His head is alive, but his body is withered.

So, Nicole met her totem, her dream spirit guide, for the first
time. They were not afraid of each other. The Serpent made no threatening moves toward her and her feeling for him appeared to be of
curiosity rather than fear. Nevertheless, she noted his weakness: his
body was withered.

I explored with her how the Serpent, as totem, represents "life and
death."[4] Each molting symbolically represents death and the promise
of new birth. When the Snake is molting, it is lethargic, allowing the
old to give way to the new. To die is to be reborn! Even the earth has to
die in the fall and lay fallow in the winter to give way to the spring and
summer, in an endless cycle of life / death / resurrection. It was at this
point Nicole said she *knew* her physical health was failing.

Nicole was a firm believer in angels as messengers. She did not
experience any conflict between angels and totems as both messengers
and guardians. On the contrary, she was grateful that both were available to her and watching over her in spirit. She believed that when her
time had come she would see her angel and her totem would be close
by. She spoke of the fatigue she was experiencing, but she attributed
this to the medications she was taking. When she spoke of the chain
of events that was slowly unfolding in her life, she was careful to
emphasize the word "future" in our many discussions about life and
death. Nonetheless, the Serpent had come to stay and presented himself once again in a most horrifying way:

> I am outside walking in a creek. The water is waist high. I
> see a box. There are cherries in the box and I hear
> sounds from inside the box, like bees perhaps. I jiggle
> the lid and a snake comes out. He comes toward me.
> Then a second snake comes out. I grab them to keep
> them from biting me. I hold tight. I have them firmly in
> my hands near the neck to keep them from biting. They
> have enormous fangs. They are hissing and struggling. I
> think to throw them but, no, I cannot kill them. I wake up.

Nicole's Totems Appear

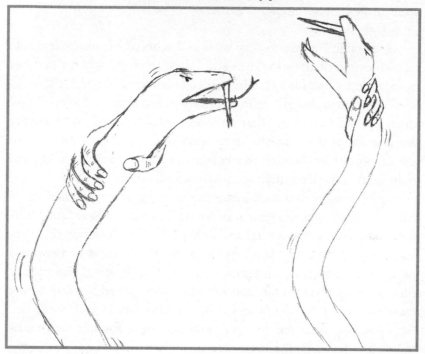

Nicole and I spent some time analyzing the message about death and the other world in this dream of the Serpent totems. There were cherries in the box that housed the serpents until Nicole's discovery and ultimate release of the serpents. The symbolic meaning attached to fruit is "immortality."[5] Her totems had come to warn her that it was time. Nicole did not yet yield. She wanted to "hold on" until she was too weak.

Soon after these dreams, Nicole's condition worsened and she was admitted to intensive hospital care. Whenever she requested it, I came to her bedside and this appeared to be comforting to her. She was eventually released to her home, but she could not manage and reluctantly she and the Kitty Girls relocated to her sister's home to be provided for in a caring, loving environment. When she could, she worked diligently to record on paper the image of her Serpent totem as she experienced it in her dreams.

Although Nicole was very weak and in hospice care, she was able to walk some of the time, but still I was surprised when I saw her name on my scheduled appointments. I contacted her and offered to visit her at home, but she insisted on being seen in my office one more time. She had a dream to share and she wanted to share it in the safety and comfort of the room she knew and loved, even though she needed the support of her brother to manage the walk into the building and even to sit in the chair that was so familiar to her.

After we greeted each other she went on in a calm manner. "I have seen my angel and I am at peace with myself and my fate. I look forward to seeing my mother and father." Nicole felt certain that they were waiting patiently; she was like a ship that sails away from one port, away from the loving arms of her brothers, sisters and friends, only to meet adventure in another land. She looked forward to the loving arms of her mother and father awaiting her arrival.

She had finalized her will and arranged for her service of farewell. Afterward, she requested there be people, food, music and partying. "There has to be laughter and fun," she declared. She had arranged with hospice that she would be alert and not so sedated that she did not know what was transpiring around her. "If need be, will you come to me when it is time?" she requested. "Of course I will come!" I replied. Then she shared one of her last dreams with me:

> I am healed, strong and vibrant. I stand tall and go
> confidently into the future yet unknown. I am fearless.
> You see, my totems are my escorts. They are the sacred
> healers and guides. I am safe and happy.

Nicole could not kill the serpents. She knew that they were her totems and were only doing their job: informing her of the nearness of the hour of her death. Finally, in the last dream of which she spoke, those very same serpents were her escorts, upright, proud and sure of the journey they would travel together. Nicole noted the serpents at her feet and her lack of fear of them. Finally, Nicole traveled with her totem escorts: strong, sure, free and fearless. Her earthly cares were no more.

Away I Go!

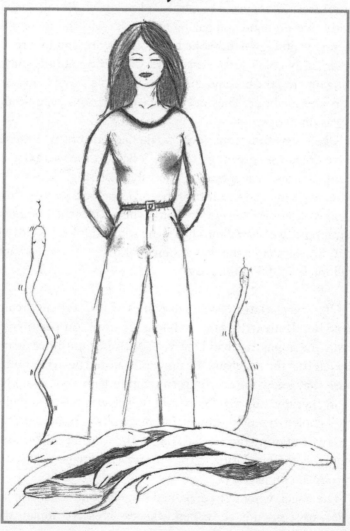

A few days before she died, Nicole requested a home visit from me. Her family and her best friend were there, keeping vigil. I was struck with the beauty of the room that her family had prepared for her last days. She lay beside a window which looked out on a grassy, tree-lined landscape. She could see the wild animals and birds that visited during the day and the stars at night since the home was located in a rural area. There was a fireplace and a mantel. Sitting on the mantel, with chin on hand and gazing at Nicole, was the most beautiful angel, just waiting patiently. She had golden wings and wore a lovely white dress. Nicole's Kitty Girls were wandering about, sometimes jumping up onto the bed and checking on Nicole's well-being, at other times roaming about. They did not leave the room even though the door was often open.

Nicole was fully conscious, weakened but not uncomfortable. After we exchanged greetings, I asked, "Nicole, have we said it all yet?" She replied, "Yes." I suggested: "Then shall we sing?" She smiled and together we sang the beautiful song of hope and wonder from the classic movie *The Wizard of Oz*: "Somewhere Over the Rainbow." She was smiling as we neared the end of the song and she fell into a gentle sleep. Only days later she was at her final rest, but she had achieved peace long before that final day.

A few weeks later, Nicole's drawings of the Serpent dreams that foretold her death arrived by mail. In a separate compartment of the box was the angel that had kept vigil with her until her death. Her family felt that the angel and the drawings should be in my possession, because they knew the drawings were intended to complete Nicole's work in therapy. I do not know whether it was Nicole's will or her family's choice to send the angel, but perhaps she or her family members viewed offering the angel to honor the journey Nicole and I had traveled together as closure to the process. (An image of this statuette is reproduced on page 218.)

The angel, whom I have named Angelica, now sits atop a bookcase near my computer and patiently keeps vigil as I complete the tasks of the day. She is a reminder of the function and purpose of psycho-dynamic psychotherapy and the dream work inherent in the process: to inform and guide the dreamer in her quest to be all she can be; in this case, informing Nicole of the tasks she had to master to rise above old wounds, fears and anger in the quest for personal autonomy and simultaneously preparing her for the journey to her final destination.

Nicole's early experience of being abused and witnessing the abuse of her brothers and sisters had traumatized her. Even after she had matured in years, she could not handle negatives. She was argumentative and rigid in her interactions with staff and administrators while also being the victim. She felt unloved and unlovable. She had very low self-esteem and she couldn't get to a place where she could co-exist with others.

In this situation, one only feels worthy if others give praise. In the course of her therapy, Nicole was able to integrate the experience of childhood and interact positively with staff and family, making good use of reason and logic. She was able to fight with determination to get what was rightfully hers in her failed marriage. The positive feedback which she earned by changing her own attitudes and behavior and allowing herself to heal served to reinforce more meaningful interactions. She learned to accept her own militant ways of surviving as valid defenses and to determine honestly whether they were useful to her. She accepted that they were no longer useful and she matured in a most impressive way.

Nicole did not complain, nor did she give up and give in until she was ready to do so. She mourned the time she would not have with her family, friends and Kitty Girls but not morbidly. She had a ready smile that was genuine all the way to the end. She became a philosopher of sorts and, with humor, mused about the strange turn of events: being named director when she was obviously terminally ill, going to Europe while in the process of chemotherapy and traveling to the home of her ancestors at such a late stage of her illness. She would not have had it otherwise.

In the end, she was the one offering sage advice and comforting words to her family and friends. She had truly become a wise woman, centered and at peace with herself. She had completed her journey and accepted her fate with courage. Nicole lived just under seven years after she was diagnosed with cancer. Her life is a testament to the hard work and courage it took to live life to the fullest, all the way to the end.

In Nicole's Words:

During our last visit together, I asked Nicole to describe what had transpired for her on her sacred journey toward individuation and what it meant to her. Without a moment's hesitation, she replied in the same words that described her elation at reaching the mountaintop in her dream: "I triumphed!"

7.

Digestive Disorders

When Mary Anne introduced herself at our first meeting, I was shocked by her appearance. She was painfully thin and fragile. Her beautiful eyes were ringed with dark circles. She was obviously in pain and she went on to explain that she suffered with a chronic illness which had affected her digestive system since she was twelve years old. At the time she began therapy with me, she was managing to survive on strained baby food, only a little at a time. Because of her worsening condition, her physicians referred her for counseling. She confessed to me she could not recall a time when she felt comfortable in her body. In her early teens she was diagnosed and treated, but she suffered many relapses and never regained the good health she experienced before the illness began.

Mary Anne described herself as quiet and shy and, at age twenty-four, she was unmarried. She had difficulty asserting herself at home or in the workplace though she enjoyed her job in human resources. There were no problems at work that she thought worthy of mentioning. She explained that she was seeking help, because she was experiencing symptoms of depression. She told me, "I am all over the map with my feelings." She was feeling helpless and alone and was having frequent bouts of weeping for no explainable reason. She was also angry. So intense was her anger that she equated it with rage. Her sleep was restless and of poor quality; consequently, she was tired and irritable. To make matters worse, her pain had become more intense. She was desperate for help.

Mary Anne was the elder of two children. She and her sister were not close in age and had little in common. Her years before the age of ten were very vague in her memory. She seemed to have blocked them from consciousness.

When she was ten years old, her father deserted them. Her mother became the primary support for the family. The only living relative her mother had was an elderly aunt, Gracie. Gracie lived in the same area and graciously invited the family to live in her home. The agreement was, as it turned out, an even exchange: her aunt was elderly and the comfort of family in the home was reassuring to her. Even as Mary Anne mourned the loss of her father and her home, she realized that living with her Aunt Gracie was not uncomfortable and, in fact, infinitely more peaceful than the home where her parents quarreled on a daily basis. Nonetheless, there were many adjustments to make. Mary Anne was very close to her aunt and at her service when she needed help. Aunt Gracie was her best friend and confidant.

Mary Anne was deeply ashamed of the fact that she no longer had a father who lived in the home. She so much wanted to be like her friends who often spoke of their fathers. It didn't help that her father lived in the same town. Her only connection to him was speaking to him in passing on the street. He was often between jobs and an embarrassment to her. After her chance encounters with her father, Mary Anne experienced a range of emotions. She felt angry. She was sad and her stomach hurt. Her way of coping was to keep her feelings hidden. She did not speak of him to anyone, not even Aunt Gracie.

Mary Anne was an excellent student and was liked by her friends and teachers. She did not enter college after graduation, electing instead to get a job to help with the family finances. She met Ron soon after graduation and they moved in together with the intention of getting married in the future. He was employed by an advertising firm and in good standing with his company. From the outside, the picture of two young people in love and planning to marry was the perfect image of a fairy tale come true; however, on the inside, many bitter arguments were taking place.

Mary Anne and her fiancé had very different values and beliefs about the meaning of commitment. He felt there was no harm in spending a considerable amount of time with his friends after work until the early morning hours. He defended his right to come and go as he pleased. Mary Anne longed for stability in all areas of her life. The quarrels aggravated her condition to the extent that her family and physician were concerned and advised her to consider separation and therapy. She was frightened at the seriousness of her physical condition and she and Ron separated. She moved into her own apartment and created a peaceful home that reflected her own personality. Mary Anne was pleased with her new living arrangements, despite the sadness she felt at being alone. She was satisfied with her job and felt less dependent on her family for support.

As Mary Anne spoke of the events that might be contributing to her pain, I found that the underlying reason for her increasing discomfort was the recent breakup of her relationship with Ron, the man she had expected to marry. Arguments occurred every day and they were both short-tempered with each other. Because of the ongoing problems, Mary Anne had separated from Ron but, to her surprise, she could not sleep and had bouts of weeping that she could not easily control. Mary Anne was heartbroken and she didn't know why she was so upset, even as she recognized how toxic she and her fiancé were together. The relationship was making her ill.

As her therapy with me progressed, Mary Anne slowly began to improve physically. She was able to tolerate more foods and, gradually, the dark circles under her eyes disappeared. However, her newfound tranquility came to an end very soon. Ron began to contact her and pleaded with her to see him and, at least, talk things over. She wanted so much to be with him and create a home together that she agreed to see him and try to mend the relationship. Very soon after the reconciliation, Ron asked her to marry him. His house was in very poor repair and it needed considerable work to make it a home. He promised that they would work together on this project. He reasoned that it would be much easier if she moved into the house to simplify the task; after all, they were going to be married soon anyway.

However, a serious problem arose after she moved into the house with Ron. She had developed a plan to begin the necessary repairs on the house and, after an eight-hour workday, scraped, sanded and painted until she was exhausted. After Ron's workday, he socialized with his friends and, when he got home, it was too late to help her with the renovations. Whenever she complained, he promised he would be home the next day to help with the house repairs, but he never kept his promise.

At this point Mary Anne began to experience stomach pain again. She grieved for the home she had made for herself when they were separated. The home she had left seemed wonderful compared to her life with Ron. She didn't know what to do: Their wedding date was set and the arrangements were all in place, but she felt exhausted and unhappy. I increased her therapy sessions to prevent any further decline in her health. Her sleep was fitful and the dreams she related to me were alarming:

> Ron and I are on vacation at the beach. We are in the hotel room and Ron announces that he isn't very happy and not sure that we should be married. He decides that he is going to stay with our neighbor, Barbara, who lives up the beach. He leaves shortly afterwards and I decide I need to talk with him, so I start up the beach to Barbara's house. It is a bright,

sunny day and the beach is very crowded with people. I have to fight my way through the crowd.

By the time I get to the end of the beach where Barbara's house is, it has gotten dark. Her house is a very old, dark, stone house that sits on a hill with the moon behind it. There are old, stone steps that lead down from the house to the beach. At the foot of the steps is a large tree full of snakes. There are snakes all over the ground and falling on me from the tree. There are snakes of all sizes. They are all black snakes and I know they are not poisonous. There is no way to get around the pit of snakes to get to the house, so I struggle very hard to flap my arms as hard as I can and I manage to fly over the snakes and up to the house.

Barbara answers the front door and says that Ron is inside and he has told her that he is unhappy, because I do not allow him enough freedom and time for himself. He feels that I depend on him too much and if I can't take care of myself, he doesn't think I will be able to take care of any children that we have, either. Ron agrees to come out and talk to me and I explain that I understand how he feels and realize that I need to start to be more independent. He accepts that and we decide to leave to go back to the hotel, but there are baby items that Barbara has lined up and need to be carried. I worry that if I am carrying these things, I won't be able to fly over the pit of snakes, which is still at the bottom of the stairs. I know I have no other choice, so, while carrying baby items in each hand, I try very hard and am able to fly over the snakes and back down the beach.

We began our discussion about Mary Anne's dream by noting that Mary Anne had met her totem/spirit guide for the first time. The

serpents were not especially friendly—in fact, they were fearsome.
Mary Anne had to find a way to escape from them and she succeeded
this time, but if the serpents had come to warn her of danger, they
would not let up until she took charge of her life. Mary Anne's dream
was a testament to her tenacious grip on her vision of being married
and having her own home. She was willing to go to any length to
make that wish come true. In her dream, she fought her way through
the crowds and climbed the hill to the dark, desolate dwelling that
resembled the house of Dracula (the evil one who drinks the blood
of his victims). In my opinion, this relationship was sucking the life
out of her.

We spoke of yet another very important symbol in the dream:
baby clothes. Anything "baby" is a symbol for new beginnings and
"possibilities of the future."[1] Mary Anne accepted this gift and went
on her own journey, flying like the legendary Mary Poppins right over
the serpents in her way. The dream told her of the destructive nature
of her relationship and the dream also predicted her escape, but it did
not appear that it would be easy.

Mary Anne struggled with her goals of being married and having
her own home. She had many serious talks with Ron about the acute
impact the house and all it required was having on her health. His
response was the same as the response he made early in their relationship: he had the right to come and go as he pleased. Mary Anne began
to recognize the destructive nature of her relationship with Ron. She
agonized about the wedding plans already in place, the people who
had received invitations to the wedding and, most of all, the effect on
her mother who had invested so much to make this a memorable day
for her. Amidst her worry and stress, her dream guided the way:

> Ron and I are standing alone in the church at the rear of
> the aisle on the morning of the wedding. I am wearing
> my wedding dress and he is in his tuxedo. We realize
> that blocking the aisle on the way to the altar is a huge,

square table with a poisonous snake on it. We look for a way around the table, but it is not possible. Every time we get close, the snake makes a move to bite. We both agree that we cannot hold the wedding since there is no way around the poisonous snake.

Mary Anne's totem tolerated no nonsense. The terror that gripped her after this dream was so compelling that, as we explored it, she came to the conclusion that she could not marry Ron. "To marry this man is to die! That is the message of the dream!" she exclaimed. Though it was only a month before the event, Mary Anne decided to cancel her wedding. When she explained her reasons, her minister commended her on her decision and her family assured her that they preferred she not go through with the wedding rather than risk her well-being. She recognized that, if she were to be healthy in mind and body, she would have to assert herself and be aggressive in her decision. Nothing Ron said dissuaded her now and she did not falter. She returned her wedding gifts along with apologies to her guests and, when all the necessary adjustments had been made, she felt as if a heavy load had been lifted. "I feel an incredible sense of relief," she conveyed to me. She had been through the agony of a destructive relationship and was free now.

Almost miraculously, Mary Anne's health began to improve and her newly-found, adventurous self decided to go away and recuperate. She longed for a simple life in a balmy climate where she could feel the warmth of the sun. She felt she needed this time alone for her body and mind to heal. Understandably, after all she had been through, her family was not in total agreement that she should make such a drastic change.

In a dream, the symbol of the Serpent predicts change, often-times big change, and Mary Anne felt this was the case for her. Despite her family's objections, by this point Mary Anne was fearless and away she flew to an island in the sun, just as her dream predicted she would.

Mary Anne returned a year later to attend to the final days of life and burial of her best friend, her beloved Aunt Gracie. When she came by my office for a therapy session, a very different Mary Anne sat across from me in her favorite chair. She was a healthy weight and her face was glowing with enthusiasm and joy, despite the sadness of her loss. She was in the process of making yet another major life decision and was preparing to enroll in a university to complete her studies, which had been interrupted by her serious illness. I saw no evidence of the sickness or sadness that had plagued her since she was ten years old.

In the course of her therapy, Mary Anne learned to trust her body to accept solid, nourishing food. She learned to recognize that her father's problems were his problems and they had nothing to do with her. She came to understand the incredible sacrifices her mother had made to provide for her children, leaving little time for attending to their emotional needs. Mary Anne discovered that if she were to become and remain healthy, she would have to be assertive and even aggressive, if that's what it took to solve a problem. She found that she could stand her ground and make a decision for her health despite objections to her plans. She was a survivor.

Mary Anne went on to complete her education in the healthcare field and found a satisfying job as a caregiver. Later she married and became a mother.

In Mary Anne's Words:

You once told me that if I got my head on straight, my body would be fine. That's exactly what happened. I am married to a wonderful man. I have two wonderful children, a beautiful home and a job that I love. I am happy.

8.

Anger

When Gabriella came in for her first counseling session with me I saw that her beautiful, bright smile and pleasant greetings did very little to hide her tension. Gabriella, a thirty-eight-year-old woman, was married and the mother of two children. At the time of the birth of her first child, she elected to be a full-time wife and mother to her children rather than attempting to balance her job, which could be very demanding, with parenting. She formerly worked in marketing for a large corporation. Her husband, Gary, owned his own business and provided the family with a lovely home in a peaceful suburban neighborhood. There was no pressure for her to earn income outside the home. Gabriella felt that she had made the right decision to be a full-time mom and she was happy to be available to her children.

However, I soon found out that was all she was happy about. She described herself as feeling down and upset most of the time. She loved her children and made certain that their needs were provided for and took them to all their activities in addition to being active at their schools, but her mood was depressed and angry and, sometimes, she isolated herself and would not interact with anyone, including her children. This could go on for days, she told me. At those times, she could not tolerate Gary's presence. Many times she could not even take part in a normal conversation with him when he came home from work. Even on good days, he was an annoyance to her.

Gabriella described herself as bright and resourceful. At our meeting she smiled a lot and was generally pleasant. She said she enjoyed fun times and family. She had friends she saw often, mostly other young mothers from her former workplace. She was involved in church activities and provided a well-balanced social life for her children. Outside the home, she felt relaxed as long as she was interacting with other people. Once inside the home, her mood changed and her anger and depression returned. There was nothing specific that she could identify that would support these changes in mood except Gary. When she attempted to describe her feelings about his presence, she could only say, "He's just *there!*"

At Gary's flourishing business he employed a number of people and was committed to his business interests and to his work, his employees and his family. Family was a high priority for him. He felt that he had been a good provider by funding the beautiful home where the family lived. He took care to spend time at home with his children but tended to be rather strict with them, as opposed to Gabriella's more lenient way of parenting. It seemed to me that Gary's parenting style was similar to his own childhood experience, as Gabriella described it to me.

Gary's parents were very strict and had high expectations of their children. With his own children, Gary was more likely to correct rather than guide. This was the opposite of Gabriella's experience with her own parents and she was agitated and felt irritated by his style when he involved himself with the children, especially in a parental role. Gary, she said, spoke in a logical, rational manner almost devoid of emotion. His manner of speaking and his precise way of attending to his personal needs irritated her. In short, everything about him annoyed her and she did not feel she could relate to him or his needs. Yet, she said he was a loving and caring parent and husband. She acknowledged his positive attributes but continued to insist that he was so annoying! Her mixed feelings were bewildering to her.

I asked Gabriella to tell me more about her own background after we finished discussing her husband's. Gabriella was the eldest of three children. Until she was four years old, her earliest memories were happy and fun. It was in her fourth year that her father died suddenly. She had little memory of the years following her father's death until she was ten years old. After his death her mother devoted herself to the care of the children. She never remarried. Gabriella, as the eldest daughter, helped even from early childhood as much as she could. Somehow, she knew her mother needed her despite her own tender years. Life was difficult for the family. Resources were scarce, but they were not impoverished. Then the family experienced yet another tragedy. When Gabriella was an adolescent her brother was diagnosed with an incurable illness. Fortunately, the extended family was large and available to help when it was needed in the care of her brother.

"What else do you remember about your father and his death?" I asked gently. Her earliest recollections of her father were ones of pure joy: Gabriella's father was jovial and full of song and laughter. He brought surprises, usually popsicles, for her. Together, they enjoyed the cool, refreshing popsicles and he played with her and sang songs to her: happy, catchy little songs from his own childhood. There was a swing in the backyard of their home where they played and he swung her higher and higher, both of them laughing and having so much fun!

We turned to Gabriella's mother, whom she said was solemn and short tempered at times; most of the time she was preoccupied and worried. Gabriella recalled her mother was often disapproving of her father and angry with him. This was bewildering to her. *How could anyone be angry with Father?* she wondered.

Then, suddenly, he was gone! There were no more popsicles, no more songs, no more laughter and no more fun. *Where did he go?* she kept asking herself. Gabriella's mother would not discuss him, nor would other family members. When she was eight years old Gabriella finally learned that he had died. She was inconsolable and could not understand why she had never been told. Much later she learned that her mother had felt that because of Gabriella's young age at the time of her father's death it was better that she not be told that he had died and would not be coming home anymore. The entire extended family obeyed the request of her mother and avoided any discussion concerning his death with Gabriella.

She questioned why she was not allowed to see him lying in his casket so she could say goodbye. She was angry and sad. Gabriella could not forgive her mother's decision to hide her father's death from her. It seemed as if it were yesterday that he did not come home. She grieved. She cried. She would not discuss her feelings with anyone, not even her mother. From that point on, Gabriella kept hidden in her heart the inner turmoil she felt. She entered a nearby university, earned her degree in business administration and joined the workforce after graduation, smiling the whole time. She felt this way nobody would ever guess how unhappy she was really feeling.

On the surface, all seemed to be well. Gabriella met and married Gary, fully expecting that her life would change for the better, but the sadness she had felt within her for so long began to surface. After the birth of her children, she was moody and had periods of withdrawal that lasted for days. Gary always took over the care of the children. He did not blame her but he couldn't understand what was happening to their family and why she was so unhappy. Gabriella could see the effect her behavior was having on her children and her marriage. She admitted that she needed help but refused medication. This is when she elected to try therapy instead.

When she first came to me, Gabriella was focused on the dismal state of her marriage. She was dissatisfied and bitter, even though she had plenty of material possessions, Gary was helpful and available, her children were excelling and wonderful, her family and friends were supportive and she had the respect of her church and community. To her, her dark moods were increasing and lasting longer than before. She knew that the children were being affected by them. "How do I stop them?" she queried me.

I explored with Gabriella my observation that she seemed to be comparing Gary with her father even though they were polar opposites. Her father was sparkling. He could light up a room and he lit up her life. In contrast, Gary was solid and stoic.

In our first sessions her grief was intense. Her moods worsened. Our therapy did not seem to be helping; it appeared she was coming to a point where it was possible she would lose control altogether.

Due to the seriousness of the situation, Gary requested a joint therapy session and both Gabriella and I agreed. Gary admitted that he avoided her whenever she was in her grievous state. He was reluctant to interfere and busied himself taking care of the children. If he tried to get near her, she unceremoniously ordered him to leave her alone. He did so readily, since her depression and anger made it difficult for him to be with her. In our meeting together, Gabriella shared her feelings of loss and abandonment with him and he agreed that he would not abandon her in the future.

Soon after their joint session, Gary was challenged to keep his agreement with her. The next time she withdrew, he sat with her. Angrily, she ordered him to go away, but he refused. He promised he would not speak to her or touch her but he would not go away. After applying this method for several weeks, the couple found that Gabriella's moods were of shorter duration than before, but they did not cease. My concern was she was so overcome with sadness and anger that she might become suicidal even though her children were so important to her. Then she had a dream where her totem arrived:

I am outdoors. The setting is unfamiliar to me. There is a
bridge. I attempt to cross the bridge, but I am met by
three large, black dogs that are growling and baring
their teeth at me. I am terrified.

We spoke of how dogs are known symbolically for their "faith-
fulness and protection."[1] They are also known as companions, but
what manner of dogs were these? They were not cute little poodles.
They were more like German Shepherds: fierce, protective and sometimes threatening. Truly, they were guardian dogs. On the surface, it
appeared that they were guarding the bridge. Or were they really
guarding her by preventing her from crossing the bridge? I took her
back to stories in Greek mythology, where the gates of Hades (hell)
are guarded by the three-headed dog Cerberus. "Hades," I said, "is the
resting place for the dead. There is no hellfire and damnation in Hades.
It is the place where the souls of the dead rest. No one gets in before
his or her time and no one gets out once he or she enters. This is the
nature of death. In a depressed person, a death wish can occur without
the conscious knowledge of the dreamer. It may be buried in the
unconscious, but it can be made known through the dream."

I felt it was time to be more aggressive in therapy. Without
dwelling on Gabriella's dream, I suggested that she take part in a
guided imagery exercise, a method of using her own thoughts and
imagination to make peace with her father's death. She was so frightened by her dream and the dogs that she quickly embraced the idea
of a session where this exercise would take place.

It was a quiet winter evening when we met for the guided
imagery exercise. The fireplace was glowing and the lights were
dimmed. The city skyline sparkled like brilliant stars from the windows. She was in a safe, peaceful room and she felt somewhat calm.
Through deep breathing and full body relaxation exercises, Gabriella
was able to feel more at peace and was open to begin her journey to
find her father. I told her to pick a place where she would like to be
with him. She chose the main street of her childhood hometown. She

described to me the stores, the trees and the place where she stood on the street.

"Call your father to come to you," I directed. Then Gabriella described him walking toward her. He wore a brown suit and tie, his best Sunday suit. *Perhaps the suit he was buried in*, I thought.

"He's holding out his arms to me and we're embracing as if he will never let me go," Gabriella continued. He spoke to her in a whisper and only she could hear the words. Eventually, he told her that he must go and she opened her arms to allow him to leave. He kissed her and walked down the street in the direction from which he came. He turned around, waved to her and disappeared from her sight.

After a few moments of silence, I guided Gabriella back to the present. Her eyes were brimming with tears and she cried as if her heart would break! When she regained her composure, she offered to share with me the words her father spoke to her: "He whispered that he loved me and that he would always love me." She knew now that he did not go away because he wanted to, but because it was his time to die. The life he had been given to live was spent and the end had come, despite his young age.

After this moving exercise, Gabriella's bouts of depression lessened and the time she spent consumed by dark moods was limited to perhaps once daily instead of several times in a twenty-four hour period. Her mood lightened to the extent that she was able to get through a day without having an angry outburst, but still she was struggling with many unanswered questions: What was it like to be married to her father? Would her mother be honest and share with Gabriella what her parents' marriage was like? Why was her mother so sad and preoccupied all the time? Gabriella longed for the answers. She wanted to know all that she could know, not only about her father but also about her mother. Just the thought of her parents' life together made her sad and she retreated from the world and felt isolated. Her totems warned her in her next dream of the danger of giving in to the depression:

I am walking in an open field. The dogs are walking
along with me, heads held high and staring straight
ahead. I somehow know not to pet or touch them. There
is no bridge, just an open field.

I explored with her that her totems were not playful dogs that
ran and romped in the field. They were guardians, come to keep her
safe and warn her of the danger of giving in to her sadness. They
would tolerate nothing less than a turnabout from the sadness and
grief that depleted her energy and drained the life from her family.
They were not about to allow her to cross the bridge from this life to
the next. The totems wanted to ensure that death would not come to
her by her design. The totems would see to that.

The next task I assigned to Gabriella was a delicate one. Given
her preoccupation with the relationship between her father and
mother, I urged Gabriella to speak with her mother about the unanswered questions that plagued Gabriella. She could not be sure that
her mother would be honest with her, but she had many questions.
Would her mother still want to protect her and hide the truth from
her daughter as she did when Gabriella's father died? We didn't know,
but for healing to occur on all levels, Gabriella had to try to find out
the answers to her questions and, if she could not, her task was to
accept that which she could not change and move on with her life.
Death was not an option for her, whether it was a spiritual or a cor-
poral death. Life was beckoning to her.

Gabriella found the courage to speak to her mother and learned
that life was difficult for her parents. Her mother told Gabriella that
she was the stable force in the family. Her father worked and left the
care of the children to his wife. He earned an hourly wage and provided a home for his family to the best of his ability. Her father was a
congenial man, happy and friendly. After his workday was over, he
enjoyed stopping at the local bar and socializing with his friends. The
problem was that when he arrived home, he usually was pleasantly

intoxicated. His mood was jovial and playful with the children, but he was of little help to Gabriella's mother, who was not enchanted by his inebriated condition. She disapproved of his drinking, but her complaints did little to change his behavior. She devoted her life to the care of her children and home and had little interest in interacting with him at these times. Gabriella remembered her mother's moods as dark and she seemed, to Gabriella, to be distant and unavailable in contrast to her father's playful moods. When he died at such a young age, Gabriella's mother valiantly kept the family intact. The extended family was ever ready to help and somehow it all worked.

The effect on Gabriella of learning new information from her mother about the family's history was profound. Having learned and faced the truth, she was ready to confront the nature of her own unhappiness. We explored together how she had been comparing Gary with her father and finding Gary wanting. She felt him too disciplined and too meticulous. His behavior was maddening! Where was the humor that she loved so much in her father? Why didn't Gary sing and dance and play? Where were the popsicles?

Like her mother before her, she was chronically unhappy with the man she had chosen to marry. Like her mother before her, she was subject to depressions so dark that they took her out of the world for days. When Gabriella realized what had occurred in her marriage, she vowed that the dark days were over. She began to look at her husband with new understanding. He had not deserted her or their children. After a day's work, he was home, ready to help with whatever needed to be done. He did not abandon her when she retreated from the world. He provided a beautiful home in a safe neighborhood for his family. What he had to give, he gave willingly. In this way, he was like her father.

I noticed Gabriella's dark moods were fewer and farther between as the months went by. She agreed. She and Gary now were communicating about everything. They dated each other again, shared jokes and laughed together. It was as though they had just discovered each other. Gabriella did not recall, even in the early days of their relationship, ever feeling so relaxed. Gary's response to all these changes was to be less concerned with details and rules and more interested in just enjoying the sunshine of life at the moment.

At this point, a miracle happened. At forty years of age, Gabriella became pregnant! Both Gary and she and their children were ecstatic. All went well medically and the pregnancy was uneventful. Gabriella gave birth to a lovely, robust baby boy. She felt as if her heart would burst with happiness. Gary's happiness was contagious. He told everybody! The children took ownership of this surprise sibling, their baby brother, and the family thrived. Gabriella had embraced life.

Gabriella was very devoted to her mother and ministered to her until her death. Even as she mourned the passing of her mother, Gabriella did not retreat from the family to grieve alone. She was very involved with her children and her community and was at peace and happy with her husband and herself at last. She could enjoy all that life had to offer and she knew that when life got rough, she could weather the storms without going into the darkness.

In Gabriella's Words:

The reason I entered into therapy was depression. The understanding I gained about my dreams and their meanings was very useful and valuable. Today, I use it to help make decisions about how to live a fulfilling, satisfying life.

9.

Panic Attacks

When I first met my client, a fifty-five-year-old, divorced woman and mother of four children, I was struck by the profound sadness reflected in her dark, brooding eyes. Her wavy hair was gathered neatly at the nape of her neck. She was casually and comfortably dressed, but she was perspiring profusely and her level of anxiety was noticeably high as she moved about trying to position herself across from me and get ready to speak.

She introduced herself as Lily and, speaking softly, began to talk of her reason for seeking therapy. She described a long history of anxiety and depression and had, in the past, engaged in psychotherapy with a professional who had decided to retire. When he closed his practice, Lily did not seek another therapist but attempted to cope with her problems without benefit of professional help.

Lily suffered from a serious health condition which was progressive in nature. She experienced days when she could not function because of the severity of her pain and discomfort. Her prescribed medications were specifically for pain, sleep disturbance and panic attacks. She began to experience panic attacks serious enough to merit treatment in the emergency room at her local hospital.

Due to the worsening of her psychological symptoms, her physician advised her to seek the services of a mental health professional. She did not heed his advice immediately, but in her follow-up visits, her physician became more persistent in his encouragement. Lily's choosing of me on this, her second attempt at therapy, was based on the time it would take to travel from her home and the fact that I was accepting new clients; otherwise the choice was random.

As I studied her, Lily's appearance and demeanor suggested a painful and profound sadness bordering on psychosis. Lily was the youngest of five children (one sister and three brothers). Her earliest memories were feelings of terror associated with abandonment and death. Subject to nightmares and an extraordinary fear of deceased people and darkness, she experienced panic reactions from an early age. Lily could not recall a time when she was not terrified, particularly of her mother. She had formed a powerful bond with her father and maintained a close and loving relationship with him until his death when she was thirty years of age.

Her relationship with her mother was conflicted. Lily was provided with nourishing food, a well-maintained home and proper grooming. Her mother's comfort level was determined by how she was viewed by her neighbors and the community. The children were encouraged to perform well in school and to keep regular attendance. Much emphasis was placed on scholarship and social conduct. To the unsuspecting eye, Lily's family portrayed a model of a well-adjusted middle-class family.

Lily's experience inside the home was quite different from the image portrayed to the neighbors. For her, her mother's character took on an ominous quality. Interactions between Lily and her mother were peppered with fear, anger, shame and blame. Her mother's anger knew no boundaries and Lily was physically punished, in the home and even in the presence of her friends. She was not permitted to play on a regular basis with other children after school or in the summer months. Her playtime was determined by her mother's mood on any given day. When Lily lost control and cried, her mother punished her and her siblings ridiculed her.

From childhood and beyond, Lily secretly experienced her mother as an evil queen sitting on a golden throne. The room she occupied was bolted shut with a huge bolt from which no one could escape. The atmosphere was dark and gloomy, with draperies fastened tightly so that the only sunlight that penetrated the darkness was through the seams of the draperies and the frame of the window. Lily imagined herself to be on bended knee in the service of her mother.

While her father was supportive of her, he was also dominated by her mother and did not intervene on Lily's behalf when she was ridiculed and punished. He did not correct the other children for fear that his wife's anger would be turned against him. Nonetheless, Lily adored her father. She came to understand that the relationship between her mother and father was hostile and she, being aligned with him, would also bear the brunt of her mother's anger. Lily later learned the origins of their discontent.

To make matters worse, her sister and brothers followed the example of their mother and teased Lily in ways that were terrifying. Lily developed a fear of the dark and experienced panic when she was alone in the dark. Her siblings delighted in extinguishing the lights when she was sent to an upper room or while she was in the process of using the bath. At those times, Lily screamed in terror. Her siblings then ridiculed and teased her. Their mother joined in and if Lily did not calm herself, she was subject to punishment for "acting out." A typical punishment was isolation. Lily was not permitted to watch television or have snacks at those times. She could hear the fun her family was having, but she was forbidden to make a sound.

Trapped in a cycle of terror, abuse and embarrassment, Lily

turned to her father for comfort, but he was also at the mercy of his wife's anger and he elected not to challenge her. Nonetheless, his presence and acceptance calmed her momentarily.

For a long while, Lily's father was employed as a salesman at a reputable firm and supported the family in a manner that provided a middle-class standard of living. However, he was afflicted with a serious chemical dependency and breathing difficulties. He often strayed from his marital partnership and paid little attention to his health status. He subsequently suffered a serious illness and could no longer go to work.

Lily's mother, already outraged with his behavior and lack of commitment to her, could not contain her rage when she was forced to take full-time employment to support her family. As the situation worsened, her behavior became even more erratic and vengeful toward both Lily and her father. The sight of him with Lily at his service provoked an extreme anger response in her mother. Lily was then the target for punishment. Lily subordinated her need for friendship and fun with children her own age to be with and care for her father. In her words, "I felt special just being with him."

Outside the home, Lily excelled in school and was a model student. In addition, she acquired the wisdom of the street and could fight with the best of them. Others soon learned, with due respect, not to antagonize her. She fought with gusto and made a mighty effort to protect her siblings and friends from any real or perceived threat.

Inside the home, Lily continued to be abused emotionally, physically and psychologically, even into adulthood, and this was the nature of her relationship with her family when she entered into therapy. Without a doubt, this was a toxic family situation.

In an effort to escape the family, Lily married at an early age and gave birth to four children. Surely now her life would change, she reasoned. To her horror, she had married a man who proved to be abusive, inflicting severe psychological, emotional and physical abuse upon her. Looking to her family for support was futile. By then her father was deceased and, without his support, she had no recourse but to divorce and raise her children alone.

During the day, Lily was employed in a management position. She took her job seriously and saw to the well-being of her children. Socially, she found her comfort zone in neighborhood bars and the friends who gathered there. She felt connected and had fun partying with them on weekend nights. Her friends were casual acquaintances whom she liked well enough and one man in the group took a liking to her. He had an unexplained, seemingly inexhaustible source of money. Everything he owned was extravagant, including his car, his clothing and his Cuban cigars. He was flanked by bodyguards and he told Lily he was very attracted to her. She developed a relationship with him but, in time, learned that he was deceitful, manipulative and controlling. She objected to his frequent lies and lack of commitment. Subsequently, she withdrew from the relationship. His response was to enlist the aid of their mutual friends to lobby on his behalf.

If Lily avoided his phone calls, he had the women in the group call her and promise her anything she could possibly want if she would merely communicate with him. The calls from her friends seemed innocent enough, but the message soon became clear: he wanted to talk with her. Lily found herself caught in a familiar web of seduction not unlike the pattern of her family experience. She recognized the danger of the relationships she had developed in her search for belongingness. It was at this pivotal point in her life that she sought therapy with me and conveyed this disturbing dream:

> I am on the street where I grew up, in my mother's house. She is not there. No one misses her. I have a boyfriend, an entertainer with a lot of money. People and bodyguards work for him. He is a fancy dresser and he adores me. I know that all the people who are working for him are untrustworthy. They carry guns and wear dark-colored

suits with dark hats. They never speak or smile. The females are raggedy and steal large sums of money. Cash is everywhere. I urge him to put the money in the bank. He ignores me. He has brought many presents for me and insists that we wrap them in pink paper to be opened later in his presence so that he can watch me unwrap them. He orders a limousine for us. But something is wrong: my boyfriend is on drugs provided by the women. He is paranoid. He will not let anyone else get near him. I console him and I know that we will go to a very nice restaurant and ultimately make love.

After addressing her family history, which was significant for depression, and her symptoms—nightmares, intense feelings of anger, preoccupation with seriously injuring others, inability to experience pleasure, low self-esteem and frequent periods of failure to gather the energy to prepare food and attend to her daily needs—I determined that her symptoms strongly indicated that she was suffering with clinical depression and would be most helped by a combination of antidepressants and psychotherapy.

Lily was quite upset when I suggested this treatment and politely refused to consider the idea of further medication, although she was on pills to manage her panic attacks. Her mother had suffered with depression most of her life and while Lily was aware of the possibility that hers was a serious depression, she steadfastly held to the belief that she could take charge of the problem and resolve the matter with therapy alone. She reasoned that she had managed to get through difficult problems before. I advised Lily that her problems went well beyond intervention at the talk therapy level, but she was adamantly against antidepressants. She did agree to return for one visit a week for a while.

At the scheduled hour each week, Lily arrived on time. She was often morose and suffered with disturbing thoughts that included fantasies of harming "someone" non-specific. She was terrified of all the anguished thoughts invading her mind and equally terrified of changing medications. I explained to her that if she permitted me to talk to her physician about her other symptoms he probably would add an antidepressant to the medications she was already taking. Once again she refused to consider taking an antidepressant to help her to cope. We met for a number of sessions, but I could not get her to accept my recommendations. It was time to admit defeat. I told Lily that, in her own best interests, I would refer her to another therapist for evaluation and possible treatment. Lily stood at the threshold of the open door, made eye contact with me and quite calmly said: "I'll think about it." She smiled and quietly closed the door.

When Lily returned for her next therapy session, she comfortably seated herself and simply stated that she had made an appointment with her physician. So, our odyssey into the deep waters of the unconscious began.

Loss was the underlying theme of Lily's life. She often suffered with pain so severe that she could not function. Her children and family were unsympathetic and she had no one to rely on for help or support. Her adult children's behavior toward her was disrespectful and demeaning. They had had plenty of examples of how to treat their mother from the family dynamics they had been exposed to since birth. Everyone connected with Lily's personal life was toxic.

Successful therapy is task-oriented. I told Lily she needed to eliminate the toxic people from her life. Making that big change would take courage and fortitude since she would have to rearrange her family relationships and give up so-called friends. It seemed easier to give up friends than family, so we started there. At first, she panicked at the very thought of being without a social system, but in time Lily recognized the toxicity of the man she had been dating and renamed him "Poison Man." She imagined the female acquaintances in his service to be his slaves, as in the dream she experienced. She knew that she did not want to be anybody's slave. Nonetheless, she would miss the date nights, the dinners at fine restaurants and the camaraderie of the local bar.

Lily had been living on an emotional merry-go-round since her earliest recollections of her past. It seemed she was anxious, depressed, angry, frightened, frustrated or grieving all of her life. The only places she could act rationally and logically were in the classroom as a child and in the workplace as an adult. In these situations, she was a respected student and a valued employee. Only when Lily was at school or at work did she feel validated and in control. However, when she left those safe settings, she broke down and was subject to very strong emotions that overwhelmed her. "When we are overcome by emotions," I said to Lily, "we cannot see clearly and tend to act spontaneously. Good judgment is rarely available to us when we are emotionally charged."

The method I suggested to eliminate Poison Man and his "slaves" from her life was to ignore all calls and communications from them. I instructed her to erase voice messages without listening to them and to screen all calls. She was to delete all "caller unknown" calls along with the familiar numbers of Poison Man and his followers. I directed her to find another activity, even if it was simply reading a book or watching a television program, and to refrain from going to the familiar bar where the "poison people" congregated.

Lily was frightened and anxious, realizing that this was yet another loss in her lifetime of losses, but she understood that, in the quest for healing, change was necessary. Lily indicated openness to the possibility of change and readied herself to do her job. She understood that she was to apply the same principles that she used at work to her daily life.

This was easier said than done! Even though Lily and I practiced how she should keep from answering the phone when her caller ID showed one of the poison people, she could not help herself from answering. Afterwards, when she realized that her friends were being used by Poison Man, she had a grief reaction, isolated herself and would not respond to anything. She did not keep her appointments with me for two weeks. On the third week, when she did attend, she was tired and sad but vowed that she could do the task. She needed all the encouragement she could get and her family's incessant calls did not help the situation. Lily was overwhelmed with emotion but in no danger of harming herself or anyone else, despite her fantasy of hurting someone. She had no one in particular in mind. Such fantasies invaded her mind at times of serious, painful grief. We discussed that disowning her friends and Poison Man was only the first step toward releasing herself from the poison people in her life.

She recognized that her family also fit into that category and this added to her terror of abandonment. I counseled her that there was no immediate plan to leave her family. When the first task was completed, then we would address her family situation. Distancing herself from her family would take several steps and would not be as direct as taking leave of the poison people. I outlined the steps for shedding her toxic family so she would know what to expect. The first step would be to establish boundaries that she would be responsible to maintain. The next step would be to allow limited interaction with family members, with her in control of her own schedule of leaving when she sensed that trouble was about to begin. Eventually, she could reorganize her relationship with her family in a manner that was not dangerous to her. She would be in charge! With the other poison people, there would be no interaction, limited or otherwise, and no reconciliation—ever.

But our plans for an orderly, step-by-step exercise to move systematically away and distance herself from the family was not to be. At one level, Lily knew she had to cut ties with everyone who used and abused her, family notwithstanding, but not yet. The family's toxic effect on Lily's well-being was made known to her in her next dream:

> I am on the third floor of my mother's house. I am
> unpacking. I have many soiled clothes. They are all old

things, such as pillowcases, quilts, towels and thick things, worn and stale. It seems the room is my room. I must organize and do the laundry and freshen my bed.

Then we are all on the first floor of the house, including my grandchildren, sister and brothers. My mom is there. Then we are gathered in the dining area of the house. For no reason, I panic and jump up from a sitting position. I run to the window and I note that the glass is blackened. The window shade is drawn to the halfway mark. I peer out to see what is drawing my attention. It is bright and sunny. The grass is cut short but faded and it is brown and yellowed in spots. I look down and I see a puppy with his head pushing through the bottom of the blackened glass. I scream. He stays fast. There are more puppies on the outside ledge, one larger than the others. I hit the window and the puppies fall to the ground. The one that is halfway into the room pushes through and is followed by a bigger puppy. Then wolves jump in after them along with vicious full-grown dogs following behind. I scream and run.

As we explored her dream, Lily realized that, in her mother's house, things were not as they seemed. The blackened windows represented the unseen dangers that existed for her in that house. Lily's position in the dream was that of Cinderella. While the others chatted and socialized, Lily had to clean her room and launder the old and faded clothing. When she dared to stop and join the group socially, she was confronted with wild, primitive wolves and dogs. Her senses were acute: only she sensed the presence of the animals.

We discussed how at this point in the dream Lily was faced with the wolf in herself, which terrorized her even more. She objected to the idea that the wolf in the dream was part of her own nature. She did not want to be mean. It was better to be nice and give in and then maybe her family would like her, so she thought. Nonetheless, her task was clear. She would have to take on the nature of the wolf and, carefully, a little at a time, own her angry, hostile, biting, wolf-like nature. I conveyed that, to the extent that she would continue to preserve the Cinderella myth within herself and to the world, she would most likely continue to be troubled with the vicious, frightening landscapes which had terrorized her dreams since childhood. She felt herself going over the edge and we arranged more sessions each week to help her cope with her terror and anxiety so that her mental condition could stabilize.

Despite the consequences of inaction, the very thought of opposing the family was as terrifying as the wolves and dogs that invaded her dream. Lily came to learn that taking on her wolf-like nature was a gradual owning of her authentic self: the part of herself that could say no and mean it without guilt; the part of herself that could set limits and stick to those limits firmly and without apology. Another way to think of the task was that Lily had to be able to set boundaries. Wolves set boundaries and create order. This is the nature of the wolf totem. The wolf comes to teach that "true freedom requires discipline."[1]

That the family was dominated by their mother was indisputable. Lily's mother suffered with a respiratory condition and used the power of guilt to control and manipulate her children. Lily was especially vulnerable to the promise of a party or holiday celebration. "Would you please come? It will be so much fun," her mother begged her. She often prepared herself eagerly for the fun time her mother promised, but nothing ever changed. The parties always began in a relaxed manner, everyone being in congenial and friendly moods. Inevitably, as the event progressed, the climate changed and the familiar bickering and quarreling began. Lily could not tolerate the quarreling and she became angry and sullen. Sometimes she even cried. Her family then proceeded to blame her for spoiling the party.

After these family celebrations, Lily took refuge in her illness. She could do nothing more than take care of her hygiene needs. This breakdown in her ability to function only intensified her siblings' attacks. Her brothers and, oftentimes, her sister, began phone campaigns scolding her for spoiling the party. For Lily, there appeared to be no escape. Her physical symptoms worsened and her dangerous thoughts of hurting someone were compelling.

It was evident to me at this point that Lily's condition was now bordering on psychosis. Immediately I advised her physician of the seriousness of the situation and encouraged Lily to contact him as soon as possible for a review of her medications. I assured Lily that after she recovered from this serious relapse we would concentrate on setting limits for her and her family.

Lily's physician prescribed new medication for her; however, this led to an unexpected side effect that seriously threatened her resolve to continue with her medications. She became suspicious and preoccupied with aggressive thoughts of hurting others, as was usually the case when she became deeply depressed and immobilized. She suffered with hallucinations, the nature of which caused even familiar things to look and feel dangerous to her. She clenched her teeth to the point of pain in her jaws. She felt persecuted and was certain that people did not like her and wanted to force her out of the group that she enjoyed. The group she referred to was the weekend neighborhood tavern group (the poison people). Even under these conditions, I found her strengths were evident. With encouragement from me and her doctor, Lily worked diligently to correct the situation medically and she was successful in tolerating the adjustment. When the new medication took effect, her psychosis subsided.

It was at this point that Lily applied the term *poison* to her family members. She recognized how violently she reacted to their bullying. She agreed to learn to set limits for herself and make an attempt to avoid her part in the destructive cycle of seduction and abuse. She accepted that her response was her responsibility and gained new insight into the nature of her coping mechanism: to be sick and retreat from the world.

It was evident to me that Lily needed a social group to which she could belong and feel welcome. Together, we explored some possible means of association with a group or organization. Lily was a spiritual, religious woman with no ties to any religious community. She had always enjoyed church activities in the past. I assigned her next task of investigating religious communities with the intention of designing a social life of her own choosing, thereby breaking the codependent pattern with her family. She found a church with which she was familiar and, fortunately, her initial efforts were rewarded with acceptance and graciousness. She was excited and hopeful, yet worried and uncertain. A definite drawback was that her cousins were members of the congregation. However, she was drawn to this particular congregation and decided to explore the possibilities.

In the meantime, her family's efforts to include her in the accustomed family activities increased. She agreed to attend an event and believed that this time it would be different. She told me her brothers and her sister were really nice to her on the phone. Despite the fact that she was repeating an old, dysfunctional pattern, once again Lily attempted to be the obedient, loving daughter and attended a family gathering. I forewarned her that this was stepping into harm's way, but she elected to join the family at a holiday dinner. Even though the celebration was at a restaurant, the setting did not stop the action. In fact, in addition to blaming her, the family also referred to her as mentally ill (a new maneuver). When she began to cry with hurt and frustration they told her to see her therapist as soon as possible. After this latest interaction, Lily once again became immobilized and could not function for days. When she arrived for our next session, she shared a new, troubled dream:

> I am in Mother's house. I am sent to the basement to clean the cobwebs there. I see that the cobwebs house snakes. They are caught in the walls, on the basement

floor and in the corners. They are immobile. Mother walks down the stairs and she converses with me regarding my ability to clean the cobwebs. She walks around and then turns to leave me in the basement alone, pretending that she is going for help. I plead with her not to leave me, because I know I have to stay. Mother leaves. I am crying. The dust is overwhelming. I cry and cry! I am having difficulty breathing with the dust. There are no windows to open.

I try to knock the cobwebs from the walls and put the snakes and the dust in a plastic bag. The snakes are green and gray with a bright yellow underbelly. Some break out of the cobwebs. They try to get on me! They are attacking me! I run up the steps to the kitchen and the house is dark. I run to the living room and sit on the couch to catch my breath. A large snake comes from behind the couch and tries to bite me on the face. I struggle with him and roll off the couch and run to my room. The bedroom turns into the living room. Things move, float, crash to the floor, are switched around spontaneously and slam against each other. I know the room is possessed by the devil. In the living room, I hear a voice: "I am going to get you and there is nowhere you can run." No one hears the commotion. They are all in their rooms.

I wake up in a cold sweat. I sit up and pray. I fall back asleep and the dream continues. A voice in the living room says: "You won't be able to get in the basement again and disturb the cobwebs." I wake up, keep the light on and stay in bed. I feel that snakes are every-where in the house, that the whole house is horrifying.

This dream allowed us to access the deepest levels of Lily's experience of panic. She was beginning to learn that anything that related to her mother produced anxiety. In this dream, Lily noted that the initial experience of the totem serpents was rather benign. She had to clean the basement. This was not a new experience; she always had to clean the basement. The serpents were quiet and harmless. She was not afraid until her mother made her appearance. Then the serpents suddenly became restless and aggressive. They were so threatening that they chased her out of the basement. She ran as fast as she could, but she could not get away.

As long as Lily was not committed to changing the way she interacted within the family system, the totem Serpent was certain to torment her. The Serpent as totem is about change and to ignore its message is to invite more of the same terror. Despite her reluctance to distance herself temporarily from the family, this dream was an eye-opener for Lily. She could no longer avoid the effect that her mother's punishment, disapproval and lack of support had on her well-being. She was faced with the task of confronting the terrors of the night, owning the dream Serpent as her own and drawing from this totem the strength to release herself from her binding family ties. I encouraged Lily to begin the process of shedding her old, familiar victim skin in favor of healing and self-worth: a new skin, so to speak. Serpent medicine means the promise of a new life.

To help her gain self-confidence, we took time to make a list of her strengths and emphasize each of the gains she had made since she began therapy. I advised her to keep the list close to her and to refer to it when she felt disillusioned. As time passed she continued to add to her list. She was successful in joining a religious community and played an active role in group activities at the church. She acknowledged her role and felt comfortable in the small group environment. She had been successful in avoiding Poison Man and his followers and she no longer felt the need to frequent the local bars and associate with the people who inhabited them even though, at times, she felt lonely. Nonetheless, she was still anxious and hyper-alert.

Lily had always accepted the punishment and ridicule she

received from her family as legitimately belonging to her. She took all the blame, guilt and shame and reacted by punishing herself. Since the interactions between Lily and her mother were most often the problem that kept pushing her over the edge, I suggested to Lily she have a pretend conversation with her mother, with Lily playing both mother and daughter. This exercise was meant to help Lily understand her mother as a human being with problems of her own that had nothing to do with Lily. Lily doubted that she could express her *real* feelings toward her mother, even in a pretend situation and a safe environment, but after thinking it over, she agreed. I directed Lily to begin this imaginary conversation with her mother in which she expressed her true feelings. Lily played both parts and I intervened as therapist when I felt it was helpful:

> **Lily:** You are angry with me, because I am not catering to your whims. You are always angry with me; nothing I do pleases you. You punished me for no reason all of my life, even when I was only three. You asked me to come today and help with the laundry and I did, but all you have done is be angry and critical. You are punishing me again.
> **Mother:** You were a bad girl, that's why you were punished.
> **Lily:** You chose to beat and ridicule me and make me stay alone in a room while the rest of the family was having fun watching TV. I could not join in the fun. When I cried, everyone ridiculed me some more. What did I do that was so bad? You are never satisfied with what I do. What is it you want from me?
> **Mother:** You know that I am ill. Why are you doing this? After all I did for you! That time has gone. I am ill now and you need to be here with me. Everyone needs to be here with me.

I asked Lily to describe her mother's mood. She replied, "She is angry and critical; nothing I can do pleases her." When I asked Lily if she could remember a time when her mother was happy, Lily revealed she had no recollection before the fifth grade. "I just blocked everything out, I guess," she said. This seemed a good time of Lily's life to explore and I prompted her to reflect on her childhood and relationship with her parents.

> **Dr. S:** Tell me something about coming home from school in the fifth grade.
>
> **Lily:** Mother was always cooking. We had very good nutritious meals. Our home was spotless but dark. She did not like the sun. We were always well groomed and clean. Even the neighbors commented on our hair and clothes. We always had the latest style clothes, just like the other kids. We had chores, but I always seemed to get the hardest chores, especially the chores in the basement. That terrified me. We had fun times too, when Mother was in a good mood. We played games and watched TV and had fun. But if mother was not in a good mood, then it was a different story. She turned mean and she beat or punished me in some way or another.
>
> **Dr. S:** Could it be true that her unhappiness had another source?
>
> **Lily:** I guess so. I know that she was very unhappy with my father and me, especially me! She was mean to him too.
>
> **Dr. S:** Why was this so?
>
> **Lily:** I guess because of his drug addiction and unfaithfulness.
>
> **Dr. S:** You were married to a man who abused alcohol, mistreated you and was unfaithful, as well. Were you happy about that?
>
> **Lily:** No. I was mad.
>
> **Dr. S:** Did you find yourself scolding your children more? Were you angry more often?
>
> **Lily:** Yes. But I caught myself some years later and have not

done that for a long time. I don't do that with my grandchildren either. I don't want to be like my mother.

Dr. S: What if your mother never recognized that she was actually taking her anger out on you and anyone who offended her, real or imagined?

Lily: She would continue to do so, just like she does now. But why me?

Dr. S: Perhaps you were the most vulnerable of the children. You were the last born, were you not? Do you think we could work from that premise: that your mother's anger is all about her pain that has found a handy target in her youngest child and the anger is being directed toward you unfairly? If your mother had her way in life, what do you perceive would be the most important value to her?

Lily: She wanted to be respected in the community as a mother, wife and homemaker. She did not expect to have to go to work to support us and take care of a sick husband. She wasn't kind to him, either.

Dr. S: What stood in the way of her goals?

Lily: My father's habit of abusing drugs, unfaithfulness and illness. He couldn't work for many years. Before that, he worked every day.

Dr. S: Were you considered your father's favorite child?

Lily: Yes. He liked all of us, but he was especially nice to me.

Dr. S: So, you believe that the stage was set for you to be the object of your mother's rage because of your close bond with your father?

Lily: Yes. I can see some of it now. I loved him so, but what can I do to help myself from being so hurt and angry? Even my own children have become disrespectful and have abandoned me.

Dr. S: I think we can do a lot. You will practice *thinking* before reacting to the negative events in your life, including

anger with your mother and your children. You will soon
learn to distinguish that which belongs to you and that
which has nothing to do with you, such as your mother's
anger and depression. I will help you learn to observe people and decide if their moods have anything to do with you.
Using wolf medicine, you'll learn how to set limits for
everyone, including yourself. Then we will see if and how
the nature of your dreams changes. Remember, Serpent
medicine means change and the opportunity to renew; off
with the old skin and on with the new. Wolf medicine
means to set boundaries. You have all the tools you need to
move forward to a life of your own.
Lily: I want to believe that this can really happen.
Dr. S: You need only to try. All you need is one success and
you are on your way to healing.

Detaching from her family, even temporarily, was so hard for Lily.
Try as she might, Lily continued to stretch the limits with her family.
Once again, Lily accepted their invitation and the promise of a fun
party with her family. Unfortunately, at the party the usual events
played out. After this incident, she canceled her scheduled appointments with me and remained immobilized for days. However, during
this retreat from the world, Lily's totem was not idle. When she
returned to my office, she shared a dream that revealed the tenacity
of the Serpent totem:

> I am in Mother's house. No one is there. I have to go to the
> third floor. I hear noises, a rustling. I think there is a rat.
> I begin to search in the living room, dining room and
> Mother's room. I proceed upstairs. When I get to the
> bathroom at the top of the stairs, the windows are open.
> I close the windows and lock them. When I begin to go
> back downstairs, I see that snakes are there. They are highly
> poisonous and move swiftly. I run to the third floor and

attempt to get out the window. I am backed up against
the window. I decide to become immobile, hoping that
they will retreat. They get on me and are everywhere.
I scream the loudest scream I can and get on my toes and
run down the steps. The snakes are fast, jumping over the
banisters. I fight them. I kick, punch, hit and grab them and
throw them. They are all over me, even in my mouth.
I manage to slam them down and those I slam down die.
I have bruises from falling against the banisters, but I run
like quicksilver. The scene changes: I am at my neighbor's
garden wall, laughing and throwing up. I wake up sick to
my stomach.

When we ignore the obvious tasks ahead of us and continue to
do the same things that cause us to be mentally unhealthy, then the
spirit guides, in this case serpents, can and do become more lethal and
invasive (the snakes in Lily's mouth). Where do we begin to set limits
but with words from the mouth? The primary word Lily had to learn
was *no* and it had to be a big, lethal, no-nonsense *no*. It had to have an
element of poison in it so her family would believe her and learn to
respect her. It had to have Snake medicine behind it!

Even with snakes in her mouth, there was refuge at the neighbor's garden wall, a place where Lily could throw up and rid herself
of the poisons that lay in wait in the family home. Lily's ability to
laugh appeared to be the beginning of a new era for her—a time of
restructuring.

At once fearful and hopeful, Lily was determined that she would
start in earnest to set limits once again. She concluded that she could
no longer afford to believe the seductive invitations of her family. She
was able to accept, at least tentatively, that only she could effect change
in the family system.

I encouraged Lily to use visual aids, such as red dots, on all of
her phones; red meaning "stop," "danger," "do not answer." Setting

limits was to extend to her children and grandchildren as well. Lily was successful for longer periods of time than in her previous attempt and her sleep patterns improved. She rarely felt the need to hurt people. Other sectors of her life improved. She was enjoying her church affiliation and attracting new acquaintances. The church gave her the task of mentoring the older children at the church care center. She took this duty very seriously and she attended to each child in a responsible manner.

Lily's inner changes began to reflect themselves in her outer appearance as she took more care and dressed more fashionably and she began to attract the attention of men. Eventually she entered into a relationship with a man with whom she was previously acquainted in the distant past. The relationship proved to be bittersweet, both exciting and fulfilling and simultaneously causing her to lose some of her momentum. While this relationship did not work out as well as she hoped, she was able to remove herself from the situation before it became a serious problem for her. She grieved the loss for a time, but she did not retreat to her bed as she had previously when major disappointments occurred in her life. Lily was able to own the gains that she had made in self-confidence and self-assurance as a result of the experience. "This is progress in our therapy!" I stressed. To Lily, it was almost a miracle. Her next dream predicted change in a very meaningful way:

> My dream takes place in Mother's house. My siblings and I are in the living room, which is dark and very chilly. The corners of the room are even darker, so dark that you cannot see into them. The draperies are drawn—they are always drawn—but a little light shines through from beneath them. The sun is shining very bright outside. It is so bright it is blinding and it is white and yellow. The only other light in the room is coming from a small lamp by the couch and from the television.
>
> My sister and brothers are seemingly watching

television, but they are sneaking glances over at me. I am sitting in a comfortable chair across from them. I am sitting straight up with my hands resting on the wide arms of the chair. My feet are together, flat on the floor.

Mother comes over and stands looking down at my sister, who seems to be sick. After looking at her for a few minutes, Mother goes into all of the dark corners of the room. She is gathering up some things. She is in a very big hurry. I think that she will do whatever it takes for my sister. Mother kneels down beside my sister, who is now lying on the floor. She is not feeling well. She has passed out. I want to lift her onto the couch, but Mother says that she will do it and make her feel better. Mother drapes a big earthworm across the palm of her hand. Then she reaches into her apron pocket and pulls out a small, sharp knife. She slices the earthworm lengthwise down the part that is draped across her palm. She pulls out a substance that is gelatinous. She holds it up and examines it and, as she does this, the substance hardens a little but is still pliable. The color is a yellow-white. It reminds me of a small vertebra with a blunt arrow-shaped tip.

Mother hands me the earthworm, which is still writhing around on each end. As she hands it to me, it begins to turn into a small snake. When her hand gets close to me, the snake is coiled into a little circle. She shoves the snake into the chair with me, pushing and pushing to get the snake under the cushion of the chair. Finally, she gives up and leaves the snake in the chair with me, between my thigh and the inside arm of the chair. As she moves away from me, she says, "Here, you can have this."

Then she takes the thing she pulled out of the earthworm and starts stabbing my sister with it. She

stabs her all over her face, neck, nose, ears and hair. The
stabs are hard and vicious. Finally she stops and my
sister stands up. She straightens out her hair and
smoothes her dress. While she is doing that, mother
goes back into the dark corners of the room and puts
her things back where they were originally. I am
watching my sister and brothers. They just stare back at
me. All the time this activity is going on, the snake is
squirming around just a little bit. I say to my mother,
"Okay, yes. I will take the snake home. If it doesn't die, I'll
be glad to take it home." The snake stops squirming. For
some reason, I don't feel any fear of the snake and I
think of how afraid I used to be of snakes.

Now Lily's experience with her mother was different. There was
no terror here, only curiosity and then acceptance of the offering that
her mother had for her. The landscape of the dream was once again
in the house of Lily's mother, but usual events were put on hold in
favor of a ceremonial healing. Lily and I explored how this ceremony
took Lily to the deepest layer of her mind where big dreams happen;
back to her African roots where ceremonial healing is commonly
known as Voodoo (proper name: Vodoun). Contrary to popular belief,
"Vodoun is religious in nature and is a healing ritual."[2] Lily's mother
was the central character in the dream: She was the priestess. In ceremonies of this nature, animals are used as offerings to the gods and
to the ancestors. Lily's mother performed a healing ceremony and not
only did she heal her daughter of her illness, but she also brought forth
a baby Serpent. The Serpent was offered to Lily by her mother's hand.
The same mother who had taunted, blamed, abused and beaten the
sparkle of life and joy out of Lily held in her hands Lily's redemption
and she turned it over to Lily! When Lily accepted the Serpent, she
accepted her totem as her own.

From this pivotal point in her life, Lily began journeying the
rocky road to recovery. She experienced despair with her perceived

failures and hope with her successes in dealing with her life experiences. Her view of her life and family began to take on a new perspective. She was able to question seriously her attitude toward her family and the overwhelming feeling of guilt when she had the courage to say no. Family pressures increased tenfold when Lily refused to give in to them. Her relatives developed a non-stop campaign by way of the telephone to berate, challenge and condemn her for her decision to decline family invitations. Her phone rang incessantly and the voice messages were malicious and unpredictable, at first sweet and then suddenly denouncing her. Her cousins waited for Lily after church services to quarrel with her and blame her for her mother's illnesses. She became so distraught that she began again to fantasize about striking back by hurting somebody (but nobody in particular).

I felt she was experiencing another psychotic break. The horrific dreams were coming closer to the truth about the toxicity of her family. Lily was afraid of the truth and tried to get around the revelations any way she could, but her psyche would not be denied and she shared a new dream with me:

> I am in Mother's house, down in the basement. There are snakes there. I stand on the fourth step and watch them. Some are lethargic, some are crawling and some are curled up. My sister is there. On a pallet she has branches, grass and sticks with newspapers on top. She also has a piece of deep blue rumpled plastic. It is wet with fluid in it. She calls one of the snakes. It comes over and gets on the pallet. The head of the snake is a bit bigger than a donut hole. The snakes hold their bodies upright. They are about four feet long. They hold their heads up and my sister tosses rings on them. An albino snake gets on the pallet. It is longer than four feet. It has yellow and white on its head and dark brown and green at the end. The albino snake holds very still on the pallet and accepts the rings, holding his head up high.

It is so very dark in the recesses of the basement. I see my mother in the darkest area of the basement, standing there and disapproving. I also note a light that radiates outwards in the basement. The rings disappear after they get past the yellow on the snake. I like the snake. I think of how Mother would touch him and pet him. I go to the kitchen. Then my brother and my sister come to me saying that the snake wants and likes me. I go back to the basement. They say to pet and keep him. I refuse to touch him. On the pallet there is a thick slime. They are trying to talk me into accepting the slime. They take the snake and drape it around my shoulders with the slime. I cannot accept the slime! I am repulsed by the slime! Again they try to persuade me to take the slime. Again I refuse.

They bring the snake upstairs to the kitchen. The snake is trying to communicate with me. He has beautiful red eyes. He is smiling. He does not show his forked tongue. I am fussing with the snake and the slime. I retreat to the bathroom to try to wash off the slime. When I push open the bathroom door, the snake is there and together we go down the stairs. I know my mother is displeased with me. I will not allow the snake to get near me. Downstairs, everybody is laughing. The snake is smiling at me. I admonish the snake and tell him that I am not going to keep him. Everybody laughs as the snake drapes himself around my shoulders. Mother is sitting in a chair, solemn and sober. She wants the snake to go to her. He does not go to her and I want to tell the snake how great he is for not going to her, but I do not tell him.

I discussed with her how the appearance of these serpents was wondrous and awe inspiring. As usual, the setting was the darkest part of Lily's mother's house, the place where the trauma began and where it seemed to be abiding. Her mother was present in her dark form, disapproving of the action in the dream. However, she made no attempt to stop the ritual. The serpents appeared to know their roles. They were compliant with the ritual and allowed the rings to encircle their heads. At one point, a majestic creature, an albino Snake, impressive in its distinctive stature and color, ascended the pallet. Holding his head up high, he accepted the rings. Lily wanted to "touch him and pet him." But in order to claim him as her own, she had to submit to the slime. Even when she tried to cleanse the slime from her body, she could not escape it.

As we searched further for the meaning of the slime, we saw that Lily associated it with the slipperiness of her family's clever efforts to maintain control. Her family members could be sweet and seductive, then accuse her of being mentally unstable and ungrateful. That Lily permitted the Serpent to embrace her delicately was a major event in her encounters with it. Furthermore, Lily felt a sense of triumph over the power of her mother when the totem Serpent ignored her mother's call.

I hoped that now Lily would be more intent on distancing from her family, but actually, Lily's symptoms worsened after this dream. It was as though she sensed that the time for separation had come. She began to grind and clench her teeth. Her physical pain increased to the extent that she had to rely on prescription medications to get through the day. She retreated to her bed and could not easily move her body. Her underlying medical condition worsened and the pain was unbearable for her. I explored with her how this is so often the case: "When we fail to address our emotional problems, the body will often bear the burden of that decision." Fortunately, she was open to my suggestion that she should contact her physician for a medication evaluation. He advised her to continue on the same medications and strongly urged her to continue with her therapy as well.

At this juncture, Lily began having recurring dreams that she had experienced as a child. Recalling being singled out for punishment,

Lily was vigilant in her efforts to remain invisible to the extent that she could. Her childhood Serpent dreams reflected the terror of being noticed and if she were noticed, the punishment that she was certain was coming:

> I am in the bathroom. Then I attempt to go down the stairs. I try very hard to be very, very quiet. There is only a dim light. One bulb is out, but I can see eyes and slimy bodies. I realize that there are snakes on the stairs, hissing and striking at me. They stay off the top landing. I am terrified. When I try to go down the stairs and put my foot down, they seem to beckon to me and do not move as much. I am so afraid to step on them. Then, each time I try to go down, they become calmer. One day, they lie perfectly still and no one can hear me come down the stairs.
>
> I stopped having this dream until now. They are restless again and I am afraid.

As we communicated further, Lily understood that her purposeful descent to the bottom of the stairs was the force that caused the serpents to cooperate with her effort to reach the bottom without being discovered. She reflected on her present situation, the worsening of her physical illnesses and paranoia, and considered that as long as she put off "going down the stairs" in her quest to take ownership of her life, she would be subject to the threatening serpents in her dreams. As I explored her dream with her, she came to realize that her totem serpents were protective of her. She could get all the way to the bottom of the staircase without being heard. She recalled how their bodies had become her cushion, keeping her safe from her mother's anger.

Lily was now on the way toward gaining independence from her family. She refrained from speaking to her relatives for days at a time. Her sleep patterns improved and her paranoid thoughts abated. She began once again to assert her independence from her family's unreasonable demands. Lily had found her courage!

Lily focused on her church activities. She was successful in these endeavors and loved teaching her young adult class each week. She was highly motivated to study and develop lesson plans for her students. She attended Sunday church services regularly and was determined that her family would not dissuade her from her task, nor would they be permitted to interfere with her enjoyment of Sunday services. She proved to be professional in her teaching and record keeping. Parents complimented her on her work with the students. She was amazed at the response of the community and began to feel happy once again. The nature of her dreams reflected the change in her mood from despair to joy. For the first time, there was joy of life in her dream:

> I am baking chocolate chip cookies. There is butter and sheets of cookies; so many cookies that they are overflowing in my apartment. I am eating the batter, especially the chocolate. My grandchildren are with me and they are all covered with chocolate. We are all eating batter and cookies. I give some to the kids who are knocking at the door. I share my cookies with them. I package the cookies to give them away. I feel safe, snuggly, happy and cozy. It is a sunny day and my apartment smells so good. I wake up laughing.

Lily's success in her new teaching role was sweet. She was eager to give each student in her charge the encouragement, love and respect that she herself had never experienced. She was as a child herself in the dream: "We are all eating batter and cookies." Her days reflected this enthusiasm for life.

Lily's vitality was catching. Men noticed her upbeat spirit and approached her for dates. Lily was flattered and, at the same time, afraid of once again interacting with a man on an intimate basis. She chose to engage in a relationship. As with everything else in her life, her family members did their best to interfere with the new experience she was enjoying. Her brothers were disapproving of her and Ted, the man she was seeing. They were relentless in their intent to convince Lily that dating was not the thing to do, given her so-called "serious mental illness" (in their words).

She was trying hard to preserve her emotional stability, but she was becoming more anxious. Lily could not refrain from answering the many phone calls she received in a day, nor could she maintain limits for her family. Her mother was relentless in her attacks. Lily felt disgusted with herself for wanting her family's approval and with her mother's repeated threats of dying (a favored means of control). Lily knew her mother was not dying and that this was a favorite ploy that her mother used to reign in Lily as a child when she was disobedient. At this point, she felt destabilized in all of her relationships with the exception of her time with her grandchildren and the students in her care at the church.

The new relationship was not going well. The stress of everyday life with her family was wearing on both Lily and the man in her life. He began avoiding her and did not call for days, breaking the bond that had begun to develop early in their relationship. She recognized the symptoms and elected not to address the problem, allowing the relationship to dissolve. She was grief-stricken, angry and troubled. Her next dream certainly reflected the many ways she felt threatened:

> The grandchildren's shoes are dirty and need cleaning.
> It is dark and I can see creatures. They have two arms
> and two legs and long torsos, like space people. They
> see me. One stops to look at me. He has a bony, pointed
> chin. His eyes are large and wide with a pin dot in the
> middle. One of them bites me on the side. I grab it. It is
> a snake, dark brown and muddy. I look at the bite; it is

bleeding, but okay. I throw the snake. There it goes
again! Now they are attack animals, reptiles. When I get
to the bottom there are lizards. They are snarling. I keep
pushing them away. I am not afraid to walk through
them or to push them away. They are Martians with big
goggles and pinkish pimples. They crowd around me.
They each have a thumb and three fingers that are
bony. They do not wear clothes. I fuss with them,
challenge them, confront them. I tell them to leave. I
notice that they have wide, drooping lips. I am angry
with them now. I challenge them. They are diminishing
in strength. I walk to my mother's house and throw
them out of her house. I challenge them to clean up and
put clean sheets on the bed and leave, because I know
that they are defeated.

Once again, Lily was revisited by her inner demons and once
again, she battled with them and she triumphed. The pattern was the
same. It was not a coincidence that the task of ridding herself of the
fear she had always felt was associated with her mother's house. That
she triumphed in the end was a good signal that she could and would
achieve victory in her quest for independence. "We gain, we slip back,
we make more gains," I reassured her, "until finally we make it over
the ridge. The good news is that the gains we make are permanent
and we move forward!"

Lily's dream encouraged her to move forward aggressively by
becoming more involved with outside activities and to be "too busy"
to do any family socializing. She did so and her comfort level
improved, both physically and emotionally. Her new task, along with
the ongoing task of separation by degrees, was to develop a system
much like a diary or budget where she could account for and control
her time. Lily was an excellent organizer and monitored her budget

judiciously, so this task was not foreign to her. She had never before thought to apply these same principles to planning time. In this latest task, I directed Lily to record her destination, her means of transportation, when she would leave and when she would arrive back home. She was to follow exact schedules to keep her focused on the greater task: control of her activities and time. She agreed to this task.

Lily also seemed to have more purposeful energy after this dream. She set more limits for her family, experienced better sleep patterns and found that her mood improved. She was happy with her work assignment with the students at the church and was energized to develop creative projects for them. Her good humor attracted people and she began to be more social. She attended luncheons and enjoyed a brief vacation. Life seemed to be flowing. At times, she appeared to glow.

It was not surprising that a man would be attracted to her, given her spontaneity and passion for life. Lily became friendly with Bob, a former friend, and began a romantic relationship with him. He was attentive and pleasant with her and she derived great pleasure from having a significant other in her life. This reprise of a romantic relationship was short-lived, however. She found the demands on her to be excessive with little personal satisfaction in return. Her disappointment was bitter, but to her credit, she did not suffer defeat. She had not yet invested emotional energy in the relationship before she made the decision to end it. The importance of this decision was that she made it herself in her own self-interest, with no guilt, shame or blame attached—only relief that it was over. This was an important milestone for her.

The dynamic at Lily's church care center was undergoing rapid transformation due to staff changes. Where there had been few quarrels and differences previously, now many disagreements arose between workers and the new administrators. At first, Lily was not involved in the process of change, but eventually her program was chosen to be

among those scheduled to be disbanded. There was no explanation
offered and Lily was discouraged, even though she knew her performance with her students had been satisfactory.

Her mood changed drastically following these events. She was
depressed and her physical symptoms worsened, as they usually did
in times of distress. For Lily, her body bore the burden of her psychological pain. Nonetheless, she managed to keep from taking to her
bed and isolating herself. She was exhausted. She needed a mother. It
seemed that all the messages from her family blaming her for her
mother's problems converged and Lily's dream revealed the depths of
her despair:

> I am in Mother's house. The living room is dark. The
> maroon draperies are drawn as usual. Mother is in the
> kitchen, polishing, shining and cooking. She will not go
> to bed. The house is spotless. Lights are on in the corner
> of the basement. I hate it! Now pies are sitting there.
> Mother is busy preparing for a party. Now Mother is not
> there. I am very frightened. The basement is dark and I
> look into the darkness. The more I look the more
> frightened I get. Mother is not there. I look behind the
> maroon draperies, but she is not there either. Her
> bedroom is unused. Everything seems to be out of
> control. People are fixing breakfast. Nothing is in the
> cupboard and her stuff is gone. Her dishes and cutlery
> have been replaced with someone else's. I have to sit
> down and eat. I am fearful, waiting for Mother to call.

Lily was now bearing the guilt of her mother's illness and even-
tual death, all because she was trying to gain independence from her
family. Lily expressed anguish at the very thought of causing such a
disaster. She could not bear the pressures that were constant in her
life and she made a decision to go to her family home. The decision
was based on fear and guilt rather than a conscious need to be with

her mother or her family. Her dreams were frequent and symbolically bringing to her attention her guilt, fear, shame and blame. Her body was bearing the burden. At times of crisis, her dreams appeared to reflect the present situation while encompassing the ever-present fear and powerlessness of her childhood. Her next dream differed, because she was making her break and planning her moves. I explored with her how psyche was helping her to plan:

> I am dressed up in a tailored suit with comfortable shoes. It is Easter and I am walking, but not on Mother's street. My family comes out of nowhere. They surround me. They tell me to come and see what they bought me or they will get it and go with me. I threaten to run. My mother and sister cannot run. I take off my shoes. I run, cutting through a little cutoff, and I think I lose them. I look up at another cutoff and now I am on Mother's street. I am sweaty and laughing about being on her street. My family is waving to me to come up. I look around and there is an avenue of shops. I have a choice: the family or the avenue. I choose the avenue and start running. People say, "Don't run." I calm down. My family can never catch me. It is a sunny street. I meet a police officer. He is friendly. I look into a little window at a beautiful display, but I also look over my shoulder. I am not running and not panicking. I am planning my day. I am in a place where I can sit down and plan. I do not feel hurried. I have a paper and pen and I am planning.

We discussed the importance of planning and keeping to the plan. Set boundaries. This is wolf medicine! This meant that Lily had to be aware at all times of her plan when she attended the next family party. Lily had always created an innocent, fun family party in her mind and tried to live it out by hoping it would be happy and congenial. She came to realize that her family's pressure for her to attend these events was to keep their mother's anger and discontent focused on Lily. If Lily was not present, their mother focused on one of Lily's siblings. Even though they banded together to persuade Lily to be present, if she was not present it was everyone for him or herself.

Lily chose to attend the family holiday party and this time she had her every move planned. She took note of when the event began to turn nasty, graciously wished everyone present a happy holiday and escaped to her own home, laughing and feeling triumphant all the way there. Her next dream was a futuristic and pleasant one:

> I am going to a new place. A boy is with me. I tell my snake that we will be going to a new location and he will be going with me. My snake is smiling.

Lily was planning to move out of her present home but did not know when, where or how she would manage the move. She was frightened to move away from her familiar surroundings, but she also knew that she must make this move to improve her standard of living. We discussed how her dream and the dialogue with her totem was comforting. In fact, for the first time in her memory, she felt serene.

While she continued to wrestle with her fear of being at family events, she also planned in great detail the time she would spend with her family. For the first time ever, she felt comfortable that she would fare well at any of the holiday celebrations she chose to attend. To Lily's surprise, her family made no attempt to insult, reprimand or abuse her with unkind statements. Nonetheless, she still did not trust herself to stay beyond the allocated time she had planned in advance and always left at her scheduled time. Exhausted, she slept when her task was completed. Her dreams changed significantly from this time forward. They began to take on a different character: colorful and awesome. Her next dream, I analyzed, seemed to express that a transformation was occurring:

My grandson and I are in his dorm room. There are
clothes piled high on his bed and we seem to be trying
to get dressed for something. All of a sudden, a bug flies
around the room. The tail is a very light off-white,
almost luminescent. I scream for him to try and kill it
and then the bug settles on the clothes piled up on the
bed. The whole time, my grandson is lying back on top
of the mound of unfolded clothes. Then the bug starts
to crawl around on the pile of clothes. My grandson
turns on his side and tries to pick up the bug and just as
he touches it, the bug turns into a fat purple inch worm.
He picks up the worm and puts it in the palm of his
hand. I scream to him to put it down and not to touch it.
He then puts the inch worm on his chest as he lies on
his back and lets the worm inch its way across his chest.
He lifts his head to watch. He laughs and smiles as he
watches. The color of the fat inch worm is beautiful. The
purple is a deep, rich, purplish navy blue, with tiny
flecks of gold. It is a very dark purple and the sun that
comes in the dorm window shines on the worm and the
worm seems to sparkle. I stand there and watch him
and think how fat and beautiful the inch worm is.

Even though Lily's first response to the bug/inch worm was fear,
she quickly recovered and appreciated the beauty of the colors and
the sun shining down on it, as if in blessing. The sunlight and the beautiful colors appeared to signify that the dark period that she was experiencing was over. The image of the light falling on the worm was a
warming one and Lily awakened to a new day filled with hope and
good humor.

Lily told me about her productive days. She had lunch with
friends, shopped for her grandchildren, purchased new clothes, took
part in church activities and even went on a weekend vacation. The

lazy days of summer were upon her and she gave herself over to the goodness of life. When family issues emerged, Lily was able to distance herself and she quickly silenced her siblings by giving them no opportunity to harass her.

At this time, surprising to her, the church care center contacted Lily to offer reinstatement of her previous position as instructor for the young adult group. She carefully considered the offer. However, intuitively, she sensed that the lull in the storm was temporary and the problems that had emerged in the organization in the past were most likely to occur again in the future. She feared that she would be a casualty again and she chose not to take that risk. After careful consideration, Lily declined. Her feelings about her abrupt dismissal for no definable cause resurfaced and she grieved about the unfairness of the system. That the center was affiliated with the church she loved did not make the situation easier. She felt apprehensive about the present administrators and she felt anger and grief at losing her trust in the church that she had come to love. "If we simply listen and heed the message of the dream, we can be assured in waking life that our decisions and intuitive feelings are valid," I advised her. Her next dream pointed to her distrust of the church administrators:

> I am at my church. The rooms are cold. The floors are cold and made of huge squares of stone. The ceilings are high, domed and cathedral-like. There are no drawings on the ceilings, just a beige-like color. The seats are like in a movie theater. There are no pews. The seats are covered in dark maroon velvet. The seats are tiered. The windows start high and go up to the ceilings. They are very tall and wide. The windows have thick heavy drapes. The drapes are a deep maroon and lined with heavy cotton. The linings are a medium beige color. The drapes hang down in long pleats and the valances' pleats are diagonal, draped way down. The drapes let no light in. There are lights recessed in the

huge ceiling, but they are very dim. Everyone is going about their business working and I keep trying to get their attention. I am upset that these rooms are not supposed to be like this. They ignore me, almost like I'm not even there. They don't seem to notice the drastic difference in our church.

We are there for service and it is so cold in the church that I need a winter coat, although it is summer outside. I go from person to person trying to get them to hear me, but they are looking at me puzzled-like. I am very upset, almost to the point of tears. I keep wondering, Why can't they see that this is not how it is supposed to be? Why can't they listen to me? I feel so scared and frustrated.

The resemblance to her mother's house with the maroon draperies drawn against the sun was unmistakable in this dream. As in her mother's house, the atmosphere was bleak. Lily's feeling of disillusionment with her church was evident in this dream. This discouragement added to her doubt that anything positive could happen in her lifetime on a consistent basis. She voiced her frustration at the church membership that would not address the closing of a successful program. In my discussion with Lily, she associated the feeling of being "scared and frustrated" with her entire life experience of being drawn into situations which initially promised to be positive and affirming and ultimately became disheartening, cold and frightening. When she had taken enough time to process the events of the past few months, Lily decided to continue with her membership in the church and take part in the services that nurtured her spirit while advocating for personal and policy changes that would strengthen the church organization.

Soon after, the opportunity was upon her to take possession of a new condominium in a safer, more accessible part of the city. The condo was suitable for her and included many luxury features. The decision had to be made in a few days and Lily took the plunge. She signed on the dotted line and prepared to move.

This was to be a new beginning with all excesses left behind. Lily tossed out items with abandon. She laughed at the many trips she made to dispose of belongings that she no longer felt she wanted in her life. Her family protested her decision to move to a new location (which meant that she would be a greater distance away from them), but she forged ahead with delight to meet her vacancy deadline.

Lily prepared herself well and moved to her new home. She tuned out her family's complaints and concentrated on her mission to prepare a home for herself that was pleasing and comfortable. Lily studied the ancient Chinese practice of Feng Shui. In her new home, she plotted and planned, trying different arrangements until she was satisfied with the visual aspect and the intuitive feelings that emerged. It had to *feel* right as well as look right. She depended on her Feng Shui books to inform her and delighted in the overall results of her efforts.

As a child, Lily had developed an unreasonable fear of people with disabilities that involved any kind of device attached to their bodies. This fear was challenged almost immediately upon moving into her new home, because several of her neighbors suffered with illnesses that required such devices. She described to me her feelings of terror and then guilt for not being able to empathize. She did not attempt to socialize or make new acquaintances. She isolated herself once again.

Given the significant gains she had made in therapy, neither of us found this acceptable. Together we discussed a series of treatments with a specialist whose expertise was in the treatment of trauma. Relieved that there might be a solution, she agreed and concentrated on working through the problem. In a very short time, Lily was her helpful, pleasant, sociable self, unafraid and forthcoming, to the delight of her neighbors. She enforced her strict limits on her family and she glowed with happiness. The next dream she revealed strongly suggested her future and her move to a new life:

I am in a different place, a house with many rooms. I go
from one room to another. They are nice rooms. In one
room, there is an aquarium. It is beautifully done.
Everything the fish need is there for them. There are fish
on the bottom and on the top of the water. The fish are
swimming from the bottom. They are lively and pretty.
At the top, the fish are belly-up, dull in color and their
bellies are pure white, so white they are blinding. They
turn over and I feed them. The top fish eat with the
bottom ones now. They all stay in a tight little group.

We explored how the "nice rooms" were there for her to fill with
her own life force. They were empty vessels awaiting her attention.
She felt comfortable and serene in this house of many rooms. She
noted that the fish had everything that they needed. This gave her a
feeling of pleasure. It was as if she, herself, had everything that she
needed. She had a new condo and was in the process of giving it all
that it required to become a pleasant and healthy home. She was filling
the empty rooms. In the dream, the many vacant rooms suggested
that future events in her life would most likely fill in and decorate the
rooms of her psyche.

In the dream, Lily felt the need to give nourishment to the fish
and she did so. Miraculously, the two schools of fish ate together. Lily
associated the lively fish with the potential for a new life, filled with
activity and joy. The fish that huddled together belly-up at the top of
the tank represented for her the cohesiveness of her family members
and their lack of vitality, inability to accept change and general dissatisfaction with life. Lily nourished all the fish and did not withhold
nourishment from either school, suggesting that she accepted responsibility for herself and her own past experiences with her family.
Regardless of the state of inertia and pain she had experienced, she
harbored no malice toward them.

I analyzed with her how the inert fish, lying belly-up and motion-
less, were significant. They reminded Lily that the old must die for

new life to begin. Lily's decision to relocate from her former home against her family's will appeared to be a major step toward independence. The dream landscape, with its many empty rooms and beautiful aquarium, was awaiting her move into life as an autonomous person.

Lily was moving forward both in her therapy and in her life. She got involved in the culture and activities of the community she had joined. She became acquainted with her neighbors and offered help where she perceived it was needed. Lily experienced acceptance such as she had never known before. She continued to attend her church and social events that appealed to her. She managed to keep her involvement with her family at a minimum. Her days had a rhythm that was comforting to her. Her empathy for others deepened during this period and was evident in her latest dream:

> I look out the window and notice the moon is going through the sky really fast. I point to it and ask my sister to look. She laughs at me. I think it is moving too fast and it looks very strange. This is the second time the moon has come by the window. It is coming a little faster than the first time. Now it is closer and I can see some details.
>
> Next I am standing in front of Mother's front window. The moon is really close now. It looks real scary. It is huge. I am outside looking up. The moon is going so fast you can feel it as it whizzes by.
>
> Finally, the moon gets very close and comes in very fast. All of a sudden, a sound so loud it hurts my ears pierces the silence. People run outside. The moon falls to the sidewalk. It crushes all the houses. The sidewalk is crushed and is sinking. The people are afraid and stay far back, but I am not worried or frightened. The moon is not scary anymore. It is sad and crying. I think the

moon needs help. I call the police. Help is on the way. I
feel sorry for the moon.

"Lily," I conveyed, "it is as though all the horror and terror you
have experienced in your life is encapsulated in the moon image, complete with the devastation you often felt within your family. As with
the phases of the moon, your life is a series of events that appear to
be innocent and harmless, but as each event begins to unfold, the
actions of your family become so powerful that you feel devastated
and wasted to the ground."

In the last image of her dream she was unafraid and felt only
compassion for the poor moon, which was "not scary anymore." Sick-
in-bed days were no longer an option for Lily; there was too much to
do in a day. Lily's quality of life reflected this very important change
in her attitude and ability to take life's events and unexpected changes
in stride, keeping her focus on the path toward independence and personal empowerment.

John, who was also a resident of the community, had noticed
Lily. Later he admitted that he had bided his time before making the
move to introduce himself to her. He involved himself in programs
in which she was also enrolled. He was helpful with recommendations
on how to solve a problem that she might be experiencing and managed to do his chores (laundry, etc.) at the same time she was involved
in hers. Finally, John invited her to join him for dinner and she
accepted. He and Lily began a romantic relationship based on mutual
interests. They enjoyed movies, dinners and special events together.
After an appropriate interval of time, he introduced her to his mother,
who accepted her without reservation. However, his son refused to
acknowledge Lily. John had cared faithfully for his since deceased wife
during the course of a long and debilitating illness and devoted himself
to grief and keeping her memory sacred. Even though his mother was
deceased, John's son felt that John was betraying her memory to

involve himself with another woman, despite the fact that a significant amount of time had passed since his mother's death.

Lily's children were unaware of this special relationship. She knew her family would vigorously object to any relationship that she enjoyed. Even though she was bursting at the seams to tell *somebody*, she was able to practice self-discipline (good wolf medicine). No one in her family knew of her activities since she no longer lived close enough for them to monitor her. It seemed that the empty rooms of her dream began to fill with laughter and anticipation of what the next day would bring. Her life felt full and rich. She looked forward to each new day energetically. Her health improved and her moods stabilized. If she spent a day in bed it was for reasons of rejuvenation, not because of pain and suffering.

Lily basked in the sunshine of the love that had miraculously come into her life. After a number of months in the relationship, John proposed marriage and Lily accepted. Together, they went to purchase a ring and busied themselves preparing a small, intimate wedding. The time had come to tell their families. Lily chose to share the news of her engagement with her only sister, who promptly advised her that she was obligated to inform their mother of this event. Lily agreed. She arranged a visit with her mother to share the news that she had accepted a proposal to be married. Her mother's response was predictable. She scolded Lily angrily, telling her that she was a stupid woman subject to making stupid mistakes and that if she had known of Lily's intent, she would have put a stop to the whole affair. This time, Lily was not affected by the tirade and, as graciously as she could, she excused herself and left.

Her fiancé's son was still adamantly opposed to his remarriage. In response to the negative attitudes of both their families, Lily made the suggestion that she and John elope instead of arranging a wedding in such a hostile environment. John agreed and they had great fun with the presiding judge at the ceremony. They came away giddy with excitement.

Lily's attention shifted to the home that she and her husband would share together. The dream of the house of many rooms became real in time and space. The home they chose was constructed to allow as much light into the rooms as possible. The windows were large and wide and allowed the sun to fill the space with its golden rays. Lily recalled the rays of the sun on the beautiful inch worm; it had arrived, complete with the pleasure she felt in the dream.

When I asked how she was doing at our next meeting, Lily described herself as having a perpetual smile on her face. Not only did she have a feeling of contentment but her Serpent appeared to appreciate the sunlight as well. She described him as her companion and she imagined him curling up in the light and observing her as he always did. Sometimes they quarreled and she berated him with good humor. Most importantly, the Serpent was her totem. She came to rely on him and she was peaceful and comforted in his sacred presence. Encountering the Serpent in its initially frightening form, Lily moved through fear and tolerance of it to a positive association with this powerful and compelling symbol of change. They had journeyed a long way together.

I commended Lily on the beautiful, peaceful home that she had created and affirmed that it was a testimony to the psychological changes she had accomplished. She had a new view of the world around her and her place in that world which she, herself, had created out of the chaos of her life. She had reached a place of harmony and balance between her logical, problem-solving self and her intuitive, feeling self. In her own drawings representing her journey, especially significant was a portrait on the wall of two figures, a man and a woman. Behind them was a circular backdrop, signifying the union between male and female in perfect harmony with one another, encased in the sacred center of the Divine. The Snake had its special place in the sun and, as totem, it brought its special blessings and protection to this household. (This drawing is reproduced on page 209.)

In Lily's Words:

The Beginning of the End

Well, here I am at my new therapist's building. I am so nervous, I feel as though I should run away and forget about the whole thing. I don't think I can go inside. I stand around for a few moments until people start to stare at me then I get up the nerve to go inside. I push the elevator button and wait. My heart is pounding so fast it seems as if it will burst out of my chest. When the elevator comes, I step inside and push the button for my floor. The fear has escalated and now I am sweating bullets and my stomach is in knots. I don't think I can do this! I decide that as soon as this elevator stops I am going to push the lobby button and go right back down and head for home as fast as I can.

The elevator stops and I get off. Looking around, I can see the door numbers and I can see that where I need to go is at the very end of the hall. *Oh, great!* I think to myself. *Can I get there without throwing up? Should I push for the elevator and leave? What should I do? I wish I had brought someone with me. No, no! I wanted to come by myself; I needed to come by myself, but I need someone with me. I can't do this alone. Oh, what should I do?*

Well, here goes nothing. I can't stand here in this scary hall and I don't want to waste the bus fare, so here I go. The hall seems to be a hundred feet long. Finally I reach the office door. I stand facing the door. It seems like I have been standing there for an hour. I push myself and talk out loud to myself, "Okay, go on—open the door. You don't want to be late for your first appointment, do you?" Slowly, I turn the doorknob; all the while thinking, *What is it going to be like? What will my therapist be like? Will he be mean like my other therapist? Oh, please don't be mean to me; I don't think I can bear it if he is mean to me.* While I stand there in the hall I remember how all this started with my first panic attack. It was the beginning of the end.

The Things I Learned

The first thing I learned in therapy with Dr. Strick was that *my panic attacks were not lethal*. I would not die from them. I might have to take my medications for the rest of my life and I might have to see my therapist again at certain points. I made sure to take my medications as prescribed. I went to my therapy sessions, which wasn't always easy; sometimes I couldn't get out of bed and sometimes I couldn't stop crying, but I was not going to give up. Some of my sessions were very difficult for me. Some days when I left the office I felt hopeless and sorry for myself. Then I thought about my grandchildren and that pushed me to keep going.

Next, I learned about *my ego*. It was so small and fragile when I first started my sessions: it was about the size of a tangerine. Now it is the size of a child's wading pool. Maybe that's an exaggeration, but that is the way it feels to me. I feel so good about myself and I know that I am somebody. I am intelligent, funny, pretty, outgoing and a good person. I learned that I don't have to allow people to belittle me or disrespect me anymore. I speak up for myself and I know I can do anything I try to do.

I learned about *poison people* and that *they have no place in my life*. I know how to spot them, get out of the way of them and keep them out of my life. They will bite you, inject poison into you and keep sucking at that wound. They will keep on biting you and taking your life essence away from you. I learned to get them out of my life quickly instead of letting them bite me and start to feed. Poison people can be your children, sister, mother, father, church members, friends or anybody. It doesn't matter; you still have to spot them quickly and get them out of your life before you get bitten.

"*Think about things before you speak.*" That is what Dr. Strick said to me all the time. Sometimes I talked to her about certain situations. She always asked me how I handled things and what I said. When I told her, she explained to me that I had said too much. We did roleplaying and I learned what I should have said and how I could have handled things differently. Now I know how to deal with various situations and people: what to say, what not to say, when to say something and when not to say anything.

I know now that I can't change people. They are going to be the way they are regardless, but I can change myself, stand up for myself and make sure others treat me with respect. At some point people will notice the change in me and they will modify their behavior towards me. If they don't, too bad. I just won't have anything to do with them, no matter who they are. I will stay away unless they treat me the way I expect to be treated.

I understand that I should *go for it! Be happy! Get a life! Enjoy life! Do what makes me happy!* I learned how to have a private life and to leave my children, grandchildren and my family out of my personal activities. They don't need to be involved in everything I am doing and I need to let them go live their own lives. I stand back and watch them grow and live. Instead of saying, "Oh, my grandchildren won't have anything to do with me" or "They don't come around as much as they used to," I look at them and say: "My, my, look what they have become." "Look what a good job I did nurturing them." "They are on the right path because of me." They are going to be all right, because I supported them and didn't give up.

Very importantly, I now know *I deserve to be happy!* Dr. Strick gave me a copy of an article.[3] "The Long Bag" was a great lesson for me. It was quite funny and, as I read it, I laughed a little out loud. I made copies and gave them to a few non-poisonous people in my life. The article explains that the long bag is chock full of junk that is pushed upon us at a very young age. I guess it starts as soon as you can stand up and carry your own bag. It contains a lot of dos and don'ts, names that your parents called you, put-downs, opinions and all sorts of stuff that has nothing to do with the real you. You lug this bag around all your life, continuously putting negative things in it as you go until it gets heavy and very, very long. Can you imagine how heavy the long bag can get by the time you reach my age?

I learned that the long bag was not healthy and I should drop it immediately. Let it fall right where it was and never pick it up again. It wasn't easy but I had to do it so that I could move on with my life.

I learned to be careful when choosing a man because of the different types in the world. I don't want to be abused, mentally, physically or verbally. I know now to stay away from controlling men and sexually dysfunctional men. Avoid lying men, cheating men, men who are really babies trapped in male bodies and men who want you to stroke their egos all the while they are trampling down yours. These men are sometimes very subtle and they use their dangerous skills very well. I have learned how to spot them and stay far away from them. I now know how to choose men with good track records with women and with relationships.

I learned that *I need my space*. I need time to myself. I like and appreciate my privacy. If I can have these things in a relationship then the relationship will progress. I won't feel smothered or trapped. If not, I will want to discontinue the relationship. I will flee and cut off all communications with that man. The relationship would definitely be over and *fast*. I enjoy being alone with my thoughts and there is nothing wrong with this. I enjoy thinking, reflecting and solitude.

I also learned that *I have a totem*. My totem is a Snake. In the beginning, my totem was very dark and sinister; now my totem is beautiful. I used to have these horrible dreams that frightened me so badly I woke up in a sweat, but I have learned that my totem is helpful. My totem warns me of impending danger involving other people and situations. My totem is a male. I haven't named him, but maybe I will someday. In my dreams my totem has been abused, tortured and killed among other things, but he will never go away and he will always be my totem. He reminds me of things that I have learned and if I do the wrong thing, he will let me know. Sometimes I get angry at my totem; sometimes I get tired of my totem and argue and fuss at him. Sometimes I wish my totem would go away. However, I know now that my totem is not there to frighten me. He will just be there whenever I need him.

I learned *my dreams mean things*, but not in the ways I thought they did. My explorations with Dr. Strick have made me aware that dreams can be ways of letting me know that all is not well with my life and inner being. Dreams can be warnings to me about something I may be going through. They can reveal things about my childhood. I draw pictures of my dreams and write them down. Then, with the help of Dr. Strick, we find out why I had the dreams and what they meant. The dreams may represent a problem I am going through or a situation I am in. We have explored what I thought were terrible nightmares so that I could deal with them and move on.

Lily's Totem Before Her Therapy

These are the lessons that stand out in my mind. I know they are all inside me and when situations arise they guide me and teach me all over again. I am now equipped with remedies that will allow me to do the correct and healthy things for me. These remedies will aid me in all aspects of my life whether it is social, personal, church, family gathering (if I attend) or whatever I do.

Lily's Totem After Her Therapy

The Real Beginning

The name of this story is "The Beginning of the End." I chose this title, because this is the *beginning* of my new life and the *end* of my torture. The end of being afraid, the end of being a victim and the end of being abused by other people who claim they love me. I now know what love is. It is caring, respect, happiness, sharing, togetherness and a host of other positive things. Love should make me feel good, not make me sad or make me want to kill myself. Yes, this is the real beginning for me.

Dr. Strick has informed me that my time with her is drawing to a close. She is gradually weaning me away from my sessions. I am now down—or should I say up—to one session every two weeks. This is a bittersweet victory for me. Even though I am better, I will miss our sessions. I am afraid to continue without my sessions, but Dr. Strick has assured me that, whenever I need to, I can make an appointment and see her. We both agree that I don't want to become dependent on her. I will do what I have to do and if she says it's time, then it's time, because I do trust in therapy now.

This has been a very deep experience for me and I shall never forget the first time I walked into Dr. Strick's office, the first time she spoke in that soft, gentle voice or the first words she said to me. It all seems like eons ago, but time goes on and now I have a great home, a great husband who loves me and my grandchildren are growing and thriving. They are doing good things in their lives. One has earned a scholarship to college. They are living with their mother now and when they visit they tell me they are happy. More importantly, they truly *look* happy. Life is wonderful and I am armed with all the tools and remedies I will ever need to live, grow and be contented.

Conclusion

Many symptoms inform us that something is amiss in our lives. Depression, anxiety, pent-up anger and poor physical health are but a few. These observable signs are just the tip of the iceberg that runs deep into the vast regions of the unconscious. What lies beneath the level of the conscious mind is unknown and yet that is where the real problems lie; these are often expressed in the contents and themes of our troubling dreams.

Two-thirds of those diagnosed with depression and anxiety are women. One can only guess at the number of women who suffer from anxiety and depression and have never sought help. Women face many stresses. Each year, 1.9 million women are physically assaulted, sexually abused and raped in the privacy of their homes. In the workplace, women are subjected to sexual harassment and wage and job discrimination. Women are more likely to be living in poverty with the concomitant problem of poor access to healthcare. The effects of these cumulative difficulties are feelings of powerlessness, fear, despair, poor self-esteem and anxiety, often reflected in physical illnesses for which no cause is discernible.

Additionally, a woman is most likely to be alienated from her contra sexual side, the source of reason and logic in her psyche, instead taking refuge in emotions that seem to run rampant through her consciousness. She is unlikely to be aware of her shadow side, the side that is exactly the opposite of all she knows herself to be. For example, a passive woman has active, assertive and even aggressive sides, which are unknown and unconscious. Conversely, an assertive woman has a passive side that lies dormant in the deep recesses of the unconscious. However unsavory these other sides are, they give balance to a woman's personality. Encountering one's unknown sides can be disconcerting and frightening. If a woman embraces all that she is, the ability to effect the changes necessary to right her situation will be readily available to her.

Women who are depressed and anxious are often subject to disturbing dreams of frightening natures. Terrifying dreams are most frequently experienced when an individual is at a crossroads, in a crisis state or in a chronically unhappy situation from which there appears to be no escape.

The dream that terrifies is the internal gauge that informs the dreamer that serious problems exist. Dreams can become so compelling that the dreamer is forced to concede that something is amiss. The intensity of the dream serves to pressure the dreamer to act on her own behalf, as difficult as that may seem. Often, the concurrent physical symptoms become more intense, offering yet another motivation to give attention to the issues. The benefits of attending to the message of the dreams may include, but are not limited to, alleviation of depressive symptoms, resolution of anxiety, enhanced self-esteem, feelings of personal empowerment and improved health status. While it is possible to ignore or deny the psychological and/or physical symptoms, the dream ego is persistent and will "plague" the dreamer until an effort is made to resolve the problems to the extent that they can be resolved.

The legendary phoenix is a bird that dies by setting itself on fire and, after three days, rises out of the ashes to begin life anew. This is a common theme of death and resurrection. So it is with psychodynamic psychotherapy. The old ways of being in the world must give way to the new. What is hidden in the darkness of the unconscious, when brought into the light of consciousness, seems new to us even though it has always been a part of our own psychology. We can only know all of our parts when they are brought to consciousness. The dream is the bridge between what we know and what we do not know. When psyche gives its message by way of the dream, the task is to integrate newly discovered parts into the whole of the personality, eventually creating the new phoenix, a "whole new you," so to speak.

In the experience of each woman profiled in this book, her reasons for seeking therapy were compelling; however, these surface problems were merely symptoms of the real issues that lay buried in the deep recesses of the unconscious.

Alena presented with an addiction to alcohol and a codependent interpersonal relationship that threatened her ability to manage her job and survive financially. The more serious problem that kept her dependent on alcohol and people close to her was grounded in severe sexual and parental abuse as a child. Until she brought the underlying issues to the forefront, Alena's development was paralyzed.

Molly's many years of suffering and being medicated for depression came to an end when she made the decision to search for solutions other than medication. While she assigned her sadness to her conflicted relationship with her husband, the underlying problem was her troubled relationship with her mother, whose criticisms were painful and defeating, even in adulthood. Molly was reliving this longtime experience in her marriage to a man who was critical and demanding. She had never learned to challenge authority and, unconsciously, she had assigned ultimate parental authority to him.

Katie's frustration with her professional relationships appeared to be personality conflicts with the predominantly male board members of the organization she had agreed to chair. She learned that the real problem was the conflicted relationship she had with her father. There was little difference in the way she reacted to the members of the board and the way she had always reacted to her father's negative comments.

Nicole's painful experience in the workplace caused her to seek professional help to survive the stresses she encountered on a daily basis. Nicole met every challenge with all her energy; she completed her assigned tasks, but she never advanced in pay or stature. She was quick to anger and defensive with her superiors. When Nicole realized she was unconsciously living out her lifetime battle with her abusive mother, she was able to function as a peer in the workplace instead of a rebellious child.

Mary Anne sought her physician's help for what her physician recognized to be an underlying problem contributing to her poor health. In addition to her serious health issues, Mary Anne was very dependent on her intended husband, who could not maintain a serious, committed relationship. What lay beneath the surface of this potentially dangerous situation for Mary Anne's survival was her father's early abandonment and her quest to find someone to care for her in the way only a father can. Only when Mary Anne attended to her grief over the loss of her father and took charge of her life did her relationships with men and her health status improve.

Gabriella's anger knew no bounds when she decided to attempt to find a solution for the dark moods that robbed her of a normal existence with her family. Her husband was most often the one who was the object of her anger. Hidden deep in the recesses of her unconscious was a longing for her beloved father who died when she was young. Unconsciously, Gabriella was comparing the gloriously happy, carefree experience of her early childhood relationship with her father to her real-life experience of marriage, family, children and responsibility and finding her present situation disappointing. Until she reached a resolution about the loss of her father, she could not appreciate the gifts of her husband and children and the beauty of her life.

Panic attacks and her doctor's advice to seek psychological help prompted Lily to engage in yet another round of therapy. She had little control of her life and did not have the benefit of a support system. Her family members were abusive and her friends were manipulative. The problems she was experiencing traced back to her mother's lifelong abuse. Lily had learned, from as far back as she could recall, to be powerless: a victim of anyone and everyone. Lily's task was to find her courage and learn to stand alone without depending on family or malevolent "friends" for support. Only then could she engage in healthy relationships and find her way to a fulfilling life of her own.

As we focused on each woman's dilemma, it might have seemed that her hidden problems would be easily recognized. On the contrary: They were concealed from and surprising to the women. Fortunately, everyone has a system that informs of the real state of affairs. This system is the realm of dreams, a purposeful and timely information resource. To pay attention to and act on messages from the unconscious is to change life for the better.

When the time has come for a woman to take action on her own behalf, the dream will be especially compelling. A dream gives forth its message in symbolic form and one of the most common symbols for needed change is the Serpent. The Serpent symbolizes death, birth, healing, rebirth, wisdom and transformation. If a woman resists (usually due to her feelings of fear and powerlessness), the dream Serpent becomes even more virulent, striking terror in the heart of the dreamer. As she takes up the tasks that will empower her, the dream Serpent gradually changes to become benign and reveals itself as the numinous, healing symbol of rebirth and transformation.

Many other forms of dream images, including other creatures of the animal kingdom, are suggestive of the need for changing the course of one's life. These could be predators, both human or animal, or compelling images of natural events, such as water and winds that threaten to overwhelm the individual. There is no limit to the number of spirit guides that can present themselves in the dream. Even when an animal appears in its most deadly, malevolent form, it is performing the service of calling attention to problems and, as a spirit guide, stands ready to tackle these problems with the dreamer. The dream serves as teacher and guide, revealing to the dreamer the state of affairs of the dreamer's life. Psyche points the way to the problem's solution through the use of symbols.

Symbolic language is common to all cultures and has existed as far back as early tribal societies and biblical times. The symbols that originate in the deepest layers of the unconscious are of an archetypal nature. They are well beyond our personal experiences and are particular to no one person but belong to the whole of humankind. They evoke powerful feelings that one cannot ignore and they appear at times of crisis when a dreamer is the most vulnerable. Symbols are the "words" and the action in the dream is the clue or the "push" toward addressing the problems occurring in the life of the dreamer. Through the use of dreams and their content, it is possible to access the unconscious for enlightenment and guidance. Nothing in a dream is superfluous and every dream has meaning.

The women featured in this book ventured into the murkiness of the unconscious and answered the call for change. They accepted the gifts of their totems as meaningful parts of their own psyches that had come to give them guidance. When we choose to be all we can be, there is usually resistance to the changes required. In that case, the guardian totem can and does get mean until real change occurs. Most of the women were introduced, by way of the dream, to their totems in a most horrific way. Troubled and frightened by the persistent occurrence of totems or humans who were predatory and dangerous, they were confronted with the difficult tasks at hand. The challenge of overcoming resistance to change and negotiating the rocky road to changing life circumstances is no easy endeavor. Each woman experienced relief from her troubling dreams after she resolved the problems she faced at the start of therapy. The same totem who was nasty, biting and fearsome transformed into an illuminating and helpful guide, leading to the death of the old and a rebirth into a new existence. She arises out of the ashes strong and resilient. She has given birth to a new phoenix.

Please be aware, in your own journey to self-knowledge, understanding and fulfillment, that the pathway to change is never straightforward. It twists and turns in many directions. The task is to stay the course, whether you meet demons or angels along the way in your dreams. Through understanding and utilizing the issues of their dreams, the women featured in this book bravely and resolutely weathered their storms, confronted their demons, came to resolution and went on with their lives, leaving the past behind. They traveled from powerlessness to healing and personal empowerment via their dreams. Their own words serve as testimony to the success of their journeys and will, I believe, inspire you to move forward and cause you to make peace with the past, embrace the present and, in the end, go onward to a new life. Arise as the new phoenix to inspire all who learn of your journey.

It is the hope of this author that, as you begin to plan and take your own journey, you will utilize these true stories of the dreams of the women featured in this book and face your own demons bravely, accept and honor your totems and guardian spirits and allow a therapist/teacher/guide to walk with you. Through integrating the old, painful experiences you have endured, rejoice with the birth of the new phoenix. May your journey be fruitful and blessed with peace and joy.

Angelica

COME ON OVER TO THE HEALING PLACE

Sadie E. Strick

Wounds of others,
Themselves wounded
Never seem to fade.
Their wound, our wound
Their pain, our pain
Seem to live eternally.

Let a teacher's hand and care
Wipe away the tears.
Let a teacher bind the wound
And mingle with your fears.

Let a teacher take you where
You see the sun and sky.
And with a teacher glad rejoice
When you alight and fly.

Introduction

[1] The History Guide, "Lectures on Ancient and Medieval European History," Lecture 2, http//www.historyguide.org/ancient/lecture2b.html, Revised 2006, 1.

[2] Rosalind Miles, *The Women's History of the World* (Massachusetts: Salem House, 1988), 16–17.

[3] The History Guide, "Lectures," 2.

[4] Gerda Lerner, *The Creation of Patriarchy* (New York: Oxford University Press, 1986), 89, 213.

[5] Massoume Price, "Culture of Iran: Women in Iran, the Creation of Patriarchy 3000 BC – 21st Century," http//cultureofiran.com/women_in_iran_04.html, 1, 2.

[6] "The Gods and Goddesses of Ancient Egypt," British Museum, http://www.ancientegypt.co.uk/gods/homemain.html.

[7] "Akhenaten," Encyclopedia of World Biography, 2005, Encyclopedia.com, 23 Jul. 2011, http://www.encyclopedia.com.

[8] Price, "Culture of Iran," 1, 2.

Chapter 1

1   Emma Ross, "Landmark Study on Domestic Violence," *Associated Press*, November 2005.
2   Michael Weissenstein, "Tehran's Arrests Chilling Dissent," *Associated Press*, June 2007.
3   Dina Temple-Raston, "No One Can Know I Am a Woman," *Glamour*, March 2007.
4   Business and Professional Women's Survey/USA, Pay Equity, June 2005.
5   National Institute of Mental Health, "Women are at Greater Risk for Depression than Men," National Institute of Mental Health, April 2008, www.nimh.nih.gov/health/publications/depression-what-every-woman-should-know/women-are-at-greaterrisk-for-depression-than-men.shtml (site now discontinued).

Chapter 2

1   Ted Andrews, *Animal Wise: The Spirit Language and Signs of Nature* (Jackson, TN: Dragonhawk Publishing, 1999), 31.
2   J.C. Cooper, *An Illustrated Encyclopaedia of Traditional Symbols* (London: Thames and Hudson, Ltd., 1987).

Chapter 5

1   Jean Shinoda Bolen, *Goddesses in Older Women: Archetypes in Women Over Fifty* (New York: Harper Collins, 2001), 143.
2   Jolande Jacobi, *The Way of Individuation*, translated by R.F.C. Hull (New York: Houghton Mifflin Harcourt, 1967), 58.

Chapter 6

1   Cooper, *An Illustrated Encyclopaedia of Traditional Symbols*, 194.
2   Ibid., 117.
3   "Corn: Symbol of Spirit and Identity," Flickr-Photo Sharing, May 2008, http://www.flickr.com/photos/lanemcfadden/30353847/in/photostream/.

4 Cooper, *An Illustrated Encyclopaedia of Traditional Symbols*, 146.
5 Ibid., 74.

Chapter 7
1 Cooper, *An Illustrated Encyclopaedia of Traditional Symbols*, 35.

Chapter 8
1 Ted Andrews, *Animal-Speak: The Spiritual & Magical Powers of Creatures Great & Small* (St. Paul: Llewellyn Publications, 2005), 264.

Chapter 9
1 Andrews, *Animal-Speak*, 324.
2 Mamaissii "Zogbé" Vivian Hunter-Hindrew, Hounon Amengansie, "Voudoun ('Voodoo'): The Religious Practices of Southern Slaves in America," 2007, http://www.mamiwata.com/vodoun.html.
3 Robert Bly, "The Long Bag We Drag Behind Us," in *Meeting the Shadow: The Hidden Power of the Dark Side of Human Nature*, ed. Connie Zwieg and Jeremiah Abrams (Los Angeles: Jeremy P. Tarcher, Inc, 1990).

Acknowledgements

I am indebted to the amazing women who have so willingly agreed to share their life stories with candor in the hope that women everywhere will benefit from their therapy experiences. To my mother, Mary, who taught me how to love unconditionally; to John, the father of our children, who was called home to God in his prime; to Susan, our daughter, who left us soon after to join him; to Deborah, our daughter, who is a model of courage and compassion in my life; to Georgie, Johnny, Cordelia and Chrissy, the lights of my life; to my departed siblings, Edward, Leona, John, Bernard and Viola, thanks for being a big part of my life; to my sister and best friend, Eleanor; to my late husband, Ellis Strick, whose support and faith in my ability to reach for the stars never wavered; to my family and friends who loved and supported me and tolerated my long absences from their lives in the interest of completing this work; to my coach, Kathleen Brehony, Ph.D., whose encouragement, wise counsel, patience and humor managed to make molehills out of mountains—every time; to Donald Giarrusso, Ph.D., whose guidance led me to the yellow brick road and stayed the course until that awesome day that my Ph.D. was awarded; to Lynda Katz, Ph.D., who kept vigil along that road; to Stanton Marlan, Ph.D., Jungian Analyst, for the Saturday mornings he dedicated to the study of Jungian Psychodynamic Psychology and for the informed speakers he made available to us, avid students of Jungian psychology, but most of all for his wise and caring guidance in the course of my own psychotherapeutic experience; to Kristina Bogovich, Ph.D., for our lasting and rich partnership in the practice of psychology; to Lillian Meyers, Ph.D., for her wisdom, patience, guidance and devotion to the care of the patients and staff in her charge; to Fred Leff for his patience with an almost illiterate computer student and who never failed to praise even my smallest gain in the mastery of computer language and operation; to my holistic medical team, whose wise counsel nurtured and energized me, making each day a wondrous journey into life; to Gregory Nicosia, Ph.D., whose wisdom guided and nurtured me along the way; to Joseph Ferrero for his support in the dark days, for helping with the pesky algebraic problems and for insuring my safety and well-being in my journey to the "big" city in the attempt to be all I could be (a work in progress); to my clients, past and present, whose interest in the progression of the work kept me focused on the task; to my NICABM friends (you know who you are) whose gentle challenges kept me moving along; to Stephen King for his inspirational approach to writing; and to Sherry Rosenbaum for technical support of the highest quality. I am especially indebted to Dr. Joan S. Dunphy, publisher and editor, for her wisdom, patience and wise counsel in guiding this work to completion. Special acknowledgement and gratitude to Sigmund Freud, MD, and Carl G. Jung, MD, for their lifelong dedication to the study of the human mind.